# Remembering Jamestown

# Remembering Jamestown

*Hard Questions about Christian Mission*

*Edited by*
AMOS YONG
*and*
BARBARA BROWN ZIKMUND

PICKWICK *Publications* · Eugene, Oregon

REMEMBERING JAMESTOWN
Hard Questions about Christian Mission

Pickwick Publications
An Imprint of Wipf and Stock Publishers
199 W. 8th Ave., Suite 3
Eugene, OR 97401

www.wipfandstock.com

ISBN 13: 978-1-60899-196-9

*Cataloging-in-Publication data:*

Remembering Jamestown : hard questions about Christian mission / edited by Amos Yong and Barbara Brown Zikmund.

viii + 178 p. ; 23 cm. Includes indexes.

ISBN 13: 978-1-60899-196-9

1. Missions — History. 2. Indians of North America — Missions. I. Yong, Amos. II. Zikmund, Barbara Brown. III. Title.

BV2100 .R46 2010

Manufactured in the U.S.A.

# Contents

# Contents

# Acknowledgments

Each of these essays except one was first written for and presented at the "The Missiology of Jamestown 1607 and Its Implications" consultation at Regent University, Virginia Beach, from May 27–29, 2008. The consultation was sponsored jointly by the Virginia Council of Churches of Christ (VCC), the Interfaith Relations Commission (IRC) of the National Council of the Churches of Christ, U.S.A. (NCCC), and Regent University. The editors thank the following for making the consultation and this resulting book possible:

- The Reverend Jonathan Barton, General Minister of the VCC, for all of his work coordinating the arrangements for the consultation and supporting this project in and through its many phases;

- Chief Ken Adams, Upper Mattaponi and Chief Steve Adkins, Chickahominy; The Rev. John Upton, Baptist General Association of Virginia; Bishop Peter Lee, Episcopal Church, Diocese of Virginia; Bishop Walter Sullivan ret., Catholic Diocese of Richmond; Rev. Carson Rhyne, Presbyterian Church (U.S.A.) Presbytery of the James; and the World Council of Churches for their support and sponsorship of this venture

- Dr. Shanta Premawardhana, who came alongside this project first as director of the IRC/NCCC and then contributed a chapter for addition to the volume after he accepted the directorship of the Inter-religious Dialogue and Cooperation division of the World Council of Churches in Geneva, Switzerland;

- Dr. Randall Pannell, vice-president of academic affairs at Regent University, and Dr. Michael Palmer, dean of the Regent University School of Divinity, for making it possible for the consultation to be held on the Regent University campus.

## Acknowledgments

The editors are also grateful to Charlie Collier at Wipf & Stock for his editorial oversight; to the Wipf & Stock staff—Christian Amondson, Patrick Harrison, and Raydeen Cuffe—for their working with us through the various phases of the production, publication, and marketing of this volume; and to Timothy Lim Teck Ngern, a Regent University School of Divinity graduate assistant, for his help with various aspects of the manuscript and for work on the volume indices.

# Introduction

# Using Jamestown in 1607 to Stimulate Questions about Christian Mission in 2007

Barbara Brown Zikmund

## BACKGROUND

THIS BOOK IS THE result of four conversations: (1) Conversations among representatives of Christian denominations that participate in the Interfaith Relations Commission (IRC) of the National Council of Churches of Christ in the U.S.A. (NCCC); (2) conversations between people related to mainstream church bodies that belong to the NCCC and people who are part of conservative Evangelical churches and organizations that have historically resisted affiliation with the NCCC; (3) conversations between representatives of a variety of Christian churches that are members of the Virginia Council of Churches (VCC) and Native American tribal leaders in the Commonwealth of Virginia stimulated by the 2007 400th anniversary celebration of the founding of Jamestown in 1607; and (4), conversations that resulted from an invitational consultation held in May 2008 jointly sponsored by the Interfaith Relations Commission (IRC), the Virginia Council of Churches (VCC) and the Regent University School of Divinity (RUSD).

Councils of Churches have been part of the American religious landscape for over one hundred years. They developed when Christian groups began to question the proliferation of denominations and to work more intentionally toward Christian unity. The resulting "ecumenical movement" has taken many forms: church reunions, mergers, partnerships, councils, educational programs, and collaborative service projects. Today the "ecumenical movement" helps many Christians affirm common theologies *and* appreciate historic differences.[1]

During the past several decades, longstanding ecumenical efforts to overcome differences *between* Christians have expanded into what people now call "interfaith relations." Christians are doing more than healing the divisions within Christianity; they are exploring new ways to relate to adherents of other living religious. In the past most Christians did not question their obligation to spread Christianity to "save" so-called heathen or pagan peoples. In recent years, for many Christians, questions of mission, evangelism and proselytizing have become more ambiguous. With growing religious awareness and increasing religious pluralism at home and abroad, many Christians do not know what to think about "mission" any more. As they live and work with neighbors and colleagues grounded in many other religious traditions they are confused. How can Christians share their faith without violating their neighbor? This question is central to interfaith relations.[2]

The NCCC began Christian-Jewish relations work in 1973. A Christian-Jewish Relations Committee met regularly, building relations with many Jewish bodies through the Synagogue Council of America. Its Christian-Jewish office was staffed through part-time NCCC personnel and through contracted staff. A Christian-Muslim Committee was formed in 1976 with contributed staff support from two NCCC member churches. Initially the Muslim-Christian offices were located at the Macdonald Center for the Study of Islam and Christian Muslim Relations at Hartford Seminary in Hartford, Connecticut. A Christian-Muslim Relations Committee met in various locations around the country seeking to foster regional Christian-Muslim dialogues and to develop resources for Christians engaging in relationships with Muslims. Its work was also supported by several denominations. The program efforts of both Committees (Jewish-Christian and Muslim-Christian) were sup-

1. See Ruth Rouse, et al., *A History of the Ecumenical Movement, 1517–1968*, 4th ed. (Geneva, Switzerland: WCC, 1993), and Michael Kinnamon, *The Ecumenical Movement: An Anthology of Texts and Voices* (Geneva, Switzerland: WCC, 1997).

2. See Kenneth Cracknell, *In Good and Generous Faith: Christian Responses to Religious Pluralism* (Cleveland, OH: Pilgrim, 2006).

ported by designated giving from a handful of mainstream Protestant denominations.[3]

In 1989–1990, the two relational committees were brought together into an Interfaith Relations Working Group, and in 1991 the working group became a new Interfaith Relations Commission with a single office in the NCCC headquarters in New York. The 2007–2011 Strategic Plan of the NCCC states that the Interfaith Relations Commission has three goals: (1) to strengthen churches through their engagement in Interfaith Relations Strategies; (2) to expand and deepen interfaith conversation; and (3) to strengthen and engage in the interfaith formation of Christian leadership.

Since 1991 the Commission has continued Jewish-Christian and Muslim-Christian work and expanded relationships with Buddhism and Native American religious traditions. Because many NCCC member communions have done little thinking about Christian involvement in interfaith relations, one of the first things the Commission did in the 1990s was to draft a "Policy Statement on Interfaith Relations and the Churches."[4] After several years of work the "Policy Statement" was adopted by the NCCC General Assembly in November, 1999 and commended to the churches for study and conversation.

The policy statement begins by acknowledging the changing experience of "religious diversity in our country" and how the "work of Christian unity" is "increasingly intertwined with questions regarding our relationships with those of religious traditions outside the historic Christian church." It notes that "The Americas have always been religiously plural. For millennia, their indigenous peoples have practiced their religions, diverse yet all based on respect for and connectedness with the earth and all of creation."[5] Yet, the Statement also confesses "that Christians participated in attempts to eradicate indigenous peoples and their traditional religions."[6]

---

3. A brief history of these efforts is found in the "Interfaith Relations Commission Handbook," p. 9, at http://www.ncccusa.org/pdfs/IRChandbook2008.pdf (last accessed September 17, 2009).

4. For the text of the NCCC's "Policy Statement on Interfaith Relations and the Churches," see http://www.ncccusa.org/interfaith/ifr.html (last accessed September 17, 2009).

5. "Policy Statement on Interfaith Relations and the Churches," §5.

6. Ibid., §6.

The Interfaith Relations Commission further recognizes that within Christianity there are conflicting views about mission and interfaith relations. Sometimes Christians are fearful that cultivating hospitality with non-Christians will compromise their loyalty to Jesus Christ and diminish their mission efforts. Sometimes Christians think that they can justify interfaith engagement only when it is viewed as a preliminary step undergirding mission efforts seeking conversion. Not surprisingly, interfaith partners are wary. Sometimes Christians feel that the resources and energy spent on interfaith relations could be better spent on evangelism. They insist that Jesus sent his disciples into the world to spread the Gospel in order that the world might be "saved."

The Interfaith Relations Commission understands this tension. As it has cultivated conversations with people in other religious traditions, it has also expanded conversations among Christians, recognizing that there are varied understandings of Christian mission, what scholars call "missiology."[7]

In order to strengthen its own intra-Christian conversations about missiology the IRC has recently invited representatives from ecumenical and interfaith organizations, including the Society for Pentecostal Studies, to become active members of the IRC and to participate in its semi-annual meetings.[8] In February 2006 the IRC held one of its regular meetings at Fuller Theological Seminary, a flagship Evangelical seminary with a vital school of missions. It continues to discuss new ways in which Christians with different understandings of mission and interfaith relations can expand their conversations.

In 2006, as the IRC was discussing its desire to explore more deeply the theology of missions among various Christians, the general minister of the Virginia Council of Churches (VCC), who participates in the IRC as a representative from the Ecumenical Networks Committee of the NCCC, began talking about the work of the VCC with indigenous tribal groups in the Commonwealth of Virginia. He noted that although Virginia was planning many special events in 2007 to mark the 400th anniversary of the settlement of Jamestown in 1607, there was need to

7. See Terry Muck and Frances S. Adeney, *Christianity Encountering World Religions: The Practice of Mission in the Twenty-first Century* (Grand Rapids: Baker, 2009).

8. See http://www.sps-usa.org/. It was felt that the work of the SPS was especially open to a relationship with the NCCC and depending on how that relationship went, others were projected for the future.

push anniversary programs and conversations beyond their focus upon the English colonial settlement. The settlement of Jamestown was not something that descendents of Native peoples and African slaves viewed as something to celebrate. Jamestown needed to be remembered because it led to tragedy among indigenous peoples and supported slavery in the name of Christian mission. As the Commission talked about various attitudes toward Christian mission, it became clear that Jamestown was a local case study around the issues of missiology that continue to challenge contemporary Christians. What happened in 1607 with the founding of Jamestown? How did/do Christians share their faith, or engage in mission and evangelism then and now without violating the integrity of their neighbors?[9]

In that conversation, one of the Commission members, a representative from the Society for Pentecostal Studies who teaches at Regent University School of Divinity in Virginia Beach, Virginia, suggested that Regent University might be willing to host an event on "missiology." Students and faculty at Regent, an Evangelical university founded by Christian conservative Pat Robertson, were already engaging issues of mission and would be open to conversations with representatives from the NCCC. It was an unlikely partnership, but it was exactly the kind of place where conversations might move beyond stereotypes. The idea was broached and soon an agreement was reached between the NCCC (with some involvement by the World Council of Churches), the VCC and the Regent University School of Divinity to jointly sponsor an invitational convocation on "The Missiology of Jamestown 1607 and Its Implications for 2007 and Beyond."

Names of scholars and presenters were collected, invitations extended and in May 2008 the convocation was held in Virginia Beach. The earliest description of the consultation stated that it would explore the "the missiology of Jamestown 1607, its impact on Native Americans, African Americans, and the church in the United States, and directions for missiology for a religiously and culturally diverse United States in the 21st century." Eventually several of the Native American tribes recognized

---

9. The 400th anniversary "celebration" produced several new publications—e.g., Benjamin Wooley, *Savage Kingdom: The True Story of Jamestown 1607, and the Settlement of America* (New York: Harper Collins, 2007); Bob Deans, *The River Where America Began: A Journey Along the James* (Lanham, MD: Rowman & Littlefield, 2007); and Karen Ordahl Kupperman, *The Jamestown Project* (Cambridge: Belknap, 2009).

in Virginia pledged financial support. When invitations went out they stated,

> The events of Jamestown, Virginia in 1607 inaugurated a shared history of 400 years, weaving together diverse peoples and cultures. They also mark the beginning of a long history of invasion, exploitation, and the denigration and loss of Native American land and religious traditions. In addition, Jamestown marks the first port of entry of slavery and forced migration. The commemoration of its 400th anniversary is an occasion not only to appreciate the past, but also for reflection, repentance, reconciliation and healing.
>
> What ideologies motivated these explorers? What missiologies provided church support and legitimacy to the invasion and exploitation? Are there similar missiologies that provide legitimacy to exploitations today? How do we develop missiologies that are more appropriate to the values of the gospel that are also appropriate to our present context of religious and cultural diversity in the United States?

The collection of essays in this book has been culled from the presentations shared at the consultation. They build upon hours of cross cultural and interreligious conversation. They push beyond classic missiology and use the context of colonial Virginia to present and listen to voices commonly ignored. They revisit the historic theological assumptions behind European "Christian missions" as well as contemporary tensions within Christianity about mission as "partnership or presence" and mission as "evangelism or proselytizing." They explore and recognize the historic consequences and ongoing impact of these assumptions on indigenous peoples. And finally, they invite reflection about the future of Christian mission in an increasingly pluralistic world. Although presentations about African Americans and Jamestown were part of the May 2008 consultation, this book focuses primarily upon Native American experience.

The essays published here explore diverse views of Christian interfaith relations and a variety of theological approaches to religious diversity and mission. They present insights grounded in Native American history and experience. They suggest themes for further discussions between mainline Protestants, Roman Catholics and Evangelical theologians and missiologists. Although scholarship about Christian mission history and practice often focuses on Asia and Africa, these essays do not allow the question of Christian mission to be pushed off shore. They insist that when people look seriously at the American colonial experience in Virginia there are sobering things to be remembered and overcome. Basic questions about missiology were there in 1607, although many of them were ignored and avoided. This collection of essays, revised after the May 2008 invitational consultation, seeks to stimulate honest conversation about present and future assumptions surrounding mission and interfaith engagement in our increasingly pluralistic world of the twenty-first century.

## OVERVIEW

The book is divided into four sections. Section One: Re-Visiting Native American Practices and Beliefs, begins with two essays written by Native American scholars who are highly critical of Eurocentric Christianity and its failures. Essay number one by Tink Tinker challenges the romanticism that makes Jamestown into a heroic colonial narrative. Tinker reminds Christians that their ancestors used legal and theological rationalizations to invade and conquer aboriginal lands. Tragedy, rather than romance, is a more suitable genre to remember Jamestown. The second essay by Barbara Mann argues that the cultural patterns of thinking by Christian missionaries and by Native Americans in 1607, and to the present day, were and are worlds apart. Christian cultures operate from a base of ONE, whereas Native American cultures operate from a base of TWO. Christian and Native spiritualities are mutually incomprehensible, yet colonialism resulted in the imposition of many Christian ideas on Native peoples. Today Native peoples are trying to de-Christianize their thinking and reclaim their binary views of reality.

Section Two: Re-Discovering the Concept of Discovery in the Christian Mission to Native America, has two essays exploring longstanding European legal assumptions and colonial Virginia mission attitudes. The author of the third essay, Robert Miller, a Native American legal scholar, documents how European countries that explored and colonized North America used a longstanding legal "Doctrine of Discovery" to justify European domination of indigenous peoples. This doctrine, dating back to the fifteenth century and remaining part of United States Indian policy until nearly the end of the twentieth century, assumes the superiority of European civilizations and religions and supports the goal of colonization by propagating Christianity as a means to bring "human civility" to "pagan" or "heathen" natives. Essay four, the second essay in this section, by Edward Bond, a historian of colonial Virginia, looks deeply at how colonial Virginia settlers in the early seventeenth century came to North America with many motives. Their Christianity engaged in "cultural conversion"—trying to make Natives "English" as an interim step toward the goal Christian conversion. By and large this strategy did not work. Virginia colonists also tried to convert African slaves, initially using a paternalistic argument that Christianity would make them better slaves. The result was uneven. In both efforts, however, White Christians perpetuated assumptions that African Americans and Native Americans could only be redeemed by becoming "civilized." This arbitrary mixture of colonial goals and motives did not produce desired results.

Section Three: Re-Engaging the Christian Mission to Native America, contains two essays written by evangelical Christians, yet from very different perspectives. The fifth essay is by Richard Twiss, a Lakota follower of Jesus, who writes about his own journey into Christianity and his early efforts to leave his "Indian ways" in order to be "in Christ." In disillusionment he feels that Jamestown has left a hollow legacy. Yet, he has hope in a Native-led Christian "contextualization movement." He writes that seeing Jesus as an aboriginal boy allows him to affirm the mutuality of the Trinity and the "mission of God" as community in diversity. Essay number six is by Rick Waldrop and Corky Alexander, two White Christian Pentecostals, both of whom seek to reconstruct a theology of mission rooted in the Pentecostal confidence that because the God we know through Christ is a missionary God, the life of the church must be characterized by its mission. Their essay deplores the violence and arrogance of traditional missionary efforts, and suggests that through the work of the Holy Spirit a post-Pentecostal church can be revived to offer Christian hospitality to the whole of creation.

Section Four: Re-Thinking Theology of Mission in a Multifaith World, includes two final essays pointing toward the future. Essay seven, written by Protestant theologian Shanta Premawardhana, explores the idea of a global understanding of mission drawing on mending creation and claiming a shared humanity with people of all religious traditions. It suggests that core concepts need re-thinking, such as the meaning and purpose of mission, traditional understandings of salvation, the idea of *Missio Dei*, the politics of identity, and the question of "who is at the table?" The final essay by William Burrows, a Roman Catholic, goes even further in his call for re-thinking the heritage of mission and Christian identity. He acknowledges the profound ambiguity of mission to Native Americans and upholds the insistence of Native writers like Tinker (author of the opening essay in this book) that restoring real sovereignty over the land is essential. Christian imperialism must be confronted and replaced by a "missiology of reconciliation." Mission after Jamestown needs to learn from those who have been hurt by Christendom. Only through deep dialogue between indigenous peoples and Western Christian leaders will faithful people be able to go deeply into humanity's embeddedness in creation and get beyond the idea that "what happens in Christ is mainly about spiritual transformation and eschatological hope." Authentic post Jamestown missiology, when and if it emerges, will be focused on reconciliation with all creation.

The conversations during the consultation were fruitful. Not only did the presenters interact with each other, but the audience asked good questions and engaged the issues. For some of those in attendance the honesty of the conversation was powerful. One participant wrote on his/her evaluation:

> I was very overwhelmed, in every way, throughout, and after the conversations that took place. I believe the dialogue was well needed at this point in my life with God. I was very blessed and encouraged to see that Christians and non-Christians alike are willing to talk about the difficult things that are happening and that have happened to our brothers, sisters and our nation. God has blessed this consultation.

Another wrote:

> Ideas presented were great. But still, what is the trajectory forward if we do take seriously listening to the native (presumably conflicting voices from our consultation)? It seems that we may need to get beyond the three options of accept, reject, modify. But what way forward?

In many ways the Consultation accomplished its purpose—there were conversations between Christians and non-Christians, there were conversations among Christians who rarely talk with each other, there were conversations among tribal leaders and indigenous scholars, there were conversations between Native Americans, African Americans, and Anglos, there were conversations about 1607 and 2007, and everything in between. Many of these conversations continue.

The week of the consultation a headline in a local newspaper stated "To Build Bridges Today, Religious Scholars Look Back 400 Years." It explained that "missiology" refers to church mission work, including the propagation of Christianity and the evangelization of non-Christians. It noted that cultures collided in 1607 and they continue to do so. Differences in biblical interpretation and religious priorities divide liberal and conservative Christians. Christians continue to misunderstand the thinking and practices of indigenous peoples. Yet, as the general minister of the Virginia Council of Churches put it, "Christians are all part of the same church and telling the same story, but not telling it in the same manner."[10]

Those who planned the consultation wanted to use conversations grounded in the impact of Jamestown in 1607 to stimulate questions about Christian mission in 2007 and beyond. It was intentional and in the end rather successful. The presentations and the revised essays challenge Christians from various communities and denominations to rethink their theological discourse and listen to the pain of Native Americans. Words like sovereignty, evangelism, mission, discovery, proselytize, convert, save, redeem and baptize were there in 1607, and they are still with us today. Can what happened then inform the present? What might a postcolonial theology of mission look like? At the end of the book, we note that we have confronted these hard questions about Christian mission in our pluralistic historical context. We hope that some of the proposals in these essays will survive the test of time and we share them in a spirit of humble anticipation.

10. "To Build Bridges Today, Religious Scholars Look Back 400 Years." *The Virginian-Pilot* (May 24, 2008) 5.

PART ONE

# Re-Visiting Native-American Beliefs and Practices

# 1

# The Romance and Tragedy of Christian Mission among American Indians

## Tink Tinker

*This essay attempts to challenge the usual romanticism that elevates the Jamestown story to a position of prominence in the heroic american narrative. The challenge comes by remembering two things. First of all, the Jamestown event never worked out well for the Indian people whose land was invaded. Then secondly, it is important for american people to remember that their heroic story is an amalgam of legal and theological rationalizations for invasion and conquest. To that end, the essay revisits the words of english preachers and the arguments of philosophers like John Locke, all attempting to justify the english theft of aboriginal lands on the basis of a racist denigration of those original owners of the land. Finally, the essay suggests that tragedy rather than romance might be a more suitable genre for interpreting the Jamestown story.*

## INTRODUCTION

"The only way out seems to be . . . that one voluntarily choose life-giving delusion instead of deadly truth, that one fabricate a myth." Thus spake one european master of tragic nihilism.[1] Nietzsche was attempting to

---

1. My use of the lower case for adjectives such as "english," "christian," "protestant," "catholic," "european," and "american" is intentional. While nouns naming religious, ethnic, or state groups might be capitalized out of respect for each Christian, Muslim, Abaluiya, or Jew, using the lower case "christian" or "biblical" for adjectives allows my reader to avoid any unnecessary normativizing or universalizing of the principal institutional religious or political quotient of the Euro-west. Likewise I avoid capitalizing national or regional

solve the problem of the relativism inherent in any given *present* (presumably cultural as well as temporal/historical).[2]

The original invitation I received to this consultation came close to succumbing to the usual romanticism of the colonial Self when it began a paragraph saying that Jamestown in 1607 "inaugurated a *shared history* of 400 years, weaving together diverse peoples and cultures." Taken out of its context, this is nothing more than a reference to Frederick Jackson Turner's now tired "frontier thesis" presented at the World Columbian Exhibition in 1893.[3] The incipient romantic notion is that this was a fortuitous meeting for all concerned parties. That would certainly be an example of Nietzsche's fabrication of myth. An european woman who visited Virginia and Jamestown last year on the occasion of Jamestown's quadricentennial, a woman who carries the anachronistic title of "Queen of England," averred before the Virginia General Assembly that Jamestown

---

adjectives such as american, amer-european, european, euro-western, etc., except when they are used as nouns. Apart from the reasoning already stated, it is important to my argumentation that people recognize the historical artificiality of modern regional and nation-state social constructions. For instance, who got to decide where the "continent" of Europe ends and that of Asia begins? Or are we permitted to designate the western half of north America as a separate continent clearly divided by the Mississippi River, or alternatively the Rocky Mountains? My initial reasoning extends to other adjectival categories and even some nominal categories such as *euro-* and political designations like *right* and *left*. Quite paradoxically, I know, I insist on capitalizing the w in White (adjective or noun) to indicate a clear cultural pattern invested in Whiteness that is all too often overlooked or even denied by american Whites. Moreover, this brings parity to the insistence of African Americans on the capitalization of the word Black in reference to their own community. Likewise, I always capitalize Indian and American Indian.

2. Cited from Leo Strauss, "Relativism," 13–26, in *The Rebirth of Classical Political Rationalism*, ed. Thomas L. Pangle (Chicago: University of Chicago Press, 1989) 25.

3. Turner was the key american historian at the turn of the twentieth century. He is most remembered for his "Frontier Thesis," notes the closing of the american frontier in 1893. The essay was read at the American Historical Association that year, meeting in Chicago in conjunction with the Chicago World's Columbian Exhibition. Turner's argument is that the spirit and success of the United States had been directly connected with its persistent westward expansion. As one on-line source says, "According to Turner, the forging of the unique and rugged American identity occurred at the juncture between the civilization of settlement and the savagery of wilderness. This produced a new type of citizen—one with the power to tame the wild and one upon whom the wild had conferred strength and individuality." SeeFrederick Jackson Turner, "The Significance of the Frontier in American History" (1893), available on-line at: http://www.fordham.edu/halsall/mod/1893turner.html. Cf. especially the incisive interpretation of Turner in Shari M. Huhndorf, *Going Native: Indians in the American Cultural Imagination* (Ithaca, NY: Cornell University Press, 2001) 1–78.

was important because "Three great civilizations came together for the first time—Western European, Native American and African."[4] Yet this shared history, marred by persistent acts of terrorism (and persistent pre-emptive war-making) that resulted in the death and finally in the total displacement of the aboriginal owners of the land, is a history told essentially by only one of the disputing parties. One White academic commentator responded, "That's like saying Seung-Hui Cho 'came together' with the professors and students at Virginia Tech."[5] Indeed, for American Indians the typical romanticized and sanitized history of colonialism is just as striking as this professor's comment. The killing of Indian people and the sheer theft of Indian lands dare never be concealed behind the denial of romantic memory voiced in the language of some sense of shared history. The tragedy of America's history of violence must be confronted by all the parties involved. Otherwise, the violence continues to repeat itself in our own present in a multitude of ways. Romance, in any case, merely conceals the truth of history behind a convenient façade, behind Nietzsche's fabricated myth—which turns out not to be life-giving at all. For the health and well-being of America, the truth-telling about the tragedy is more critical now than ever.

Indian people, on the other hand, are constantly being told in definitive terms that our memories of our history are heavily romanticized. When Indian people try to remember that Indian people did not much engage in warfare, White critics step in to assure us once again that Indian people had long developed "warrior" cultures, were aggressively war-like and ever blood thirsty savages. The long history of both White scholarly and popular interpretation of American Indian history, of Indian cultures, of the Indian worldview has always placarded the superiority and normativity of euro-christian Whiteness and the cultural values transported by europeans to north America. The europeans brought civilization

---

4. Queen Elizabeth II, "Address to a Joint Session of the Virginia Assembly," 3 May 2007, *American Rhetoric: On-line Speech Bank*, available at http://www.americanrhetoric.com/speeches/queenelizabethvageneralassembly.htm, (accessed June 1, 2009).

5. Ralph R. Reiland, "The 'Discovery' Racket," available at http://www.pittsburghlive.com/x/pittsburghtrib/opinion/s_507328.html. Reiland, an economics professor at Robert Morris University, calls this queen the "World's Biggest Freeloader." For those who find the analogy uneven, we need to remember the result of the 1622 Powhattan War. During the mutual celebration hosted by the english of a peace treaty that brought the war to an end, the english served a poisoned wine that killed some two hundred Indians. Then they proceeded to slaughter another fifty by hand. After signing a peace treaty.

and Christianity to backward and war-like peoples, we are told—again, Nietzsche's manufactured delusion or myth. Yet just the opposite is the actuality; european peoples brought the barbarism of european warfare and unending conquest to what had been a relatively peaceful world.[6] It is White americans who romanticize their own past in ways that falsify historical reality and engages a denial of their own history of violence.

## ROMANTICIZED HISTORY

The typical narrative remembrance of the Jamestown beachhead tends decidedly toward a romanticized heroic narrative about the White english invaders—that is, it romanticizes the colonizer Self, and does so in part by demonizing the colonized Other. It remembers, of course, the suffering of these first english colonizers as well as their heroic endurance. If the narrative treats Indian peoples at all, it is always with an eye fixed on justifying any english response to Indian irritations with their new neighbors. Indeed, this narrative tradition seems to emerge as a particular genre in any memories of colonial missionary endeavors among the aboriginal owners of the land. In many respects, these missionary memories could and should be classified with the medieval genre of hagiography, or the lives of the saints. In this sense, the narratives of european colonialism in north America fit into the larger and contemporary genre of romantic literature and into the larger landscape of european romanticism. Yet from an American Indian point of view, these stories are far from romantic and certainly not holy (hagiographic). They are much rather narratives that fit more closely into the historical european genre of tragedy. My question is: how would it change our understanding of the past to tell the narrative of american colonial history as tragedy rather than romance?[7]

---

6. In the case of Jamestown one need only recall the experience of Henry Spelman, an english survivor of the 1622 war between the english and the Powhattan Nation and who had actually lived with the Powhattans. His commentary on the military prowess of the Indian peoples the english were actively trying to displace and replace concluded: ". . . they might fight seven yeares and not kill seven men." See especially the excellent analysis of the history of Indian war-making in the first part of Tom Holm's, *Strong Hearts, Wounded Souls: Native American Veterans of the Vietnam War* (Austin: University of Texas, 1996) 26–65.

7. The inspiration for languaging my text this way comes from a fine postcolonial historiographic analysis by Jamaican anthropologist David Scott, *Conscripts of Modernity: The Tragedy of Colonial Enlightenment* (Durham, NC: Duke University Press, 2004).

What we see in the american narrative is a regular, almost normative, romanticizing of the american narrative that goes back to be beginnings of european settlement on the continent. From the beginning of the first english colony in the Americas, the progenitors of english expansionism began a process of developing a narrative that continues in several mutations to provide sustenance to contemporary american expansionism. Already by 1609, early in the Jamestown history preachers in England were ascribing "chosen people" language from the Hebrew Bible to their own english people and particularly in support of those adventurers who were participating in the invasion of another continent—at Jamestown. This chosen people metaphor, of course, was famously appropriated a couple of decades later by the Puritans at Massachusetts Bay Colony as they established their "cittie on a hill."[8]

By the time of the Jamestown beachhead in 1607, England had already learned a great deal from interpretations of the spanish colonial conquest in America. By this time England, that is the english elites, began to express its own desires and hopes for empire—and the wealth that had accrued to Spain. England already had a tensive relationship with this spanish history, of course, and Spain continued to be the major competitor that stood in the way of an english empire. To taint this competitor, England was not averse to using what they called the "black legend" of Spain's hideous and murderous reign of terror in the south, even as they developed their own dark legacy in Virginia and New England. England was, however, much more cautious to use the religious motivations and goals as cover for the economic and political aims of their adventuring. In any case, the english narrative about America and about the aboriginal owners of the land began long before their own first adventure in colonization. It came to them in the narratives used by spanish colonialists to

8. Robert Warrior, "Canaanites, Cowboys and Indians: Deliverance, Conquest, and Liberation Theology Today," in *Christianity and Crisis* 49 (1989) 261–65. See also the response to Warrior by William E. Baldridge, "Native American Theology: A Biblical Basis," in *Christianity and Crisis* 50 (1990) 180–81. Warrior argues that the Hebrew Bible Exodus story is irredeemable for American Indians because it was so mis-appropriated by europeans as they justified their invasion of America. That metaphoric misappropriation then became the foundation for everything from the religio-political doctrine of "manifest destiny" to the Monroe doctrine to our contemporary modality of the globalization of capital.

legitimize the century of spanish brutality in the south. Long before ever meeting a Native person, they already "knew" what an Indian was.[9]

Thus the first "successful" english beachhead in America was already building on a coherent narrative about America and particularly about the Native Peoples here, just as it built on the narrative of english self-importance as a budding imperial / colonial force. They had already begun to craft a narrative that represented themselves to themselves in terms of a christian theological legitimation for invasion. This legitimation typically involved three parts—a legal, an anthropological and a theological rationale. Since the initial Virginia Company Charter was concerned only with the economics of the venture, the religious / theological justification comes after the fact—at the second stage of the conquest of Indian lands, beginning in 1609, two years into the invasion and occupation. Suddenly seeing the need to rationalize their adventure with the english parliament and with the english public and particularly in order to secure the renewal of their charter, the Virginia Company began using the sermons of prominent english clergy to develop a coherent narrative that simultaneously brought together legal rationalization for the occupation along with a clear anthropological debasing of the aboriginal owners of the land (particularly described legally as non-owners!) and especially with a theological rationale that promised (but never delivered) a christian commitment to convert the Indians.

This justification was simultaneously intertwined with both a legal explanation that justified english presence in and occupation of some else's property and an anthropological description of the aboriginal owners of those lands as barbaric and somehow deserving of conquest. But as Edward Gallagher et al, have demonstrated, religious legitimation, which had been lacking in the first two years of the Jamestown colony, also very quickly became prominent in english discourse about conquest beginning in 1609.[10] Thus the narrative was from nearly the beginning intertwined

9. John F. Moffitt and Santiago Sebastián, *O Brave New People: The European Invention of the American Indian* (Albuquerque: University of New Mexico Press, 1998). This is a detailed investigation into the mis-informed stereotyping of Native Peoples in the Americas by early europeans.

10. See the very fine analytic collection essays of Gallagher and several of his graduate students treating this body of writings. Edward J. Gallagher, ed., *The Literature of Justification*, an internet publication of Lehigh University: http://digital.lib.lehigh.edu/trial/justification/about/. I have in mind here especially the collection of essays included

with and even legitimated by an english theological sense of missiology. In retrospect, as was the case with New England and the Massachusetts Bay Company more than two decades later, there is no reason to think that there was ever any actual concern for the human beings that made up indigenous communities in Virginia or in New England and who eventually finally became the target of missionary outreach. In spite of protestations to the contrary, the actual missionary outreach comes very late in both adventures. We know that John Eliot in Massachusetts seemed to have had more concern for his pagan mission wards than did the political system that commissioned his outreach—even as he was thoroughly committed to the colonization of the Indian mind (see the next section of this paper).[11]

The english narrative of conquest was couched, then, in the intertwining of both religious and legal languages that built on one another—both of which built on the anthropological debasing of Native Peoples and the political languages and political system devised by the english to legitimate their own adventuring expansionism. Religion helped explain the laws they invented; and laws helped explain and justify to the english conscience the momentary ruptures in religious coherence.[12] Even this english concern, however, voiced in theological language of missiology was already rooted in notions about english superiority and Indian inferiority that made clear the less-than character of the aboriginal inhabitants of the land.

Since the records of the Virginia Company from 1609 to 1619 are lost, there are precious few documentary resources from the early years of Jamestown itself. Moreover, there are few writings by the earliest colonial-

---

in the section titled *Jamestown—Essays*, available at http://digital.lib.lehigh.edu/trial/justification/jamestown/essay/ (accessed 2 May 2008).

11. In Massachusetts the missionary endeavor did not begin until more than a dozen years after the colony was established (well-established, as it were) when the Massachusetts General Court responded to political pressure to satisfy the english Parliament and quite some of their critiques commissioned John Eliot and provided him an annual bonus to begin the mission at Natick. See Tinker, *Missionary Conquest: The Gospel and American Indian Genocide* (Minneapolis: Fortress, 1983) ch. 1.

12. Karen B. Manahan, "Robert Gray's *A Good Speed to Virginia*," in *The Literature of Justification: Jamestown—Essays*: "Though religion and colonialism have consistently been linked, few times in history has a religious rhetoric been as persistently and effectively implemented as it was in England from 1609 to 1610." http://digital.lib.lehigh.edu/trial/justification/jamestown/essay/4/.

ists. Indeed from those who began the english beachhead at Jamestown we only have a couple of early eyewitness accounts, one written some years after the fact.[13] The only other documentary evidence for Jamestown, temporally close to the events, consists of materials written and published in England and not in Virginia, by people who had not been to America at all. Thus the earliest and largest assortment derive from the Virginia Company in England and are a good example of the colonizer's imaginary about America and its Native Peoples. Beginning in 1609 and carrying through 1610, the Virginia Company, beset with the trials of the first two years of their endeavor, began a campaign to shift public opinion in their favor in England. Concerned that their charter might not be renewed, the Company intended to press public opinion in ways that would encourage further english participation in the project. These documents consist mostly of sermons preached by very influential Church of England clergy, and they culminate at the end of 1610 with a general statement published by the Company itself.[14] All of these are a consistent attempt to justify the Jamestown project in the english mind and to win the renewal of the Company's charter.[15] An example of the emerging justification narrative for the invasion and occupation of America is this example from a sermon by Robert Gray, who described aboriginal Virginia as

> the greater part of it polluted and wrongfully usurped by wild beasts, and unreasonable creatures or by brutish savages, which by reason of their godless ignorance and blasphemous idolatrie

13. There is the slim volume written by Henry Spelman, who arrived in Virginia early in 1609 at the age of fourteen and spent his first years indentured by the colonialists to a Powhattan village. His *Relation of Virginia* was a handwritten copy left by Spelman at his death in 1623. Likewise, John Smith's heavily romanticized and politically slanted *Generall Historie of Virginia, New-England, and the Summer Isles*, was written long after his permanent return to England. He left Virginia in October of 1609, never to return (although he did make another trip to the coasts of New England in 1614. Because Smith has long been noted as an embellisher who was prone to exaggeration—especially where his own heroism becomes the subject—it is all the more important to remember when his *Generall Historie of Virginia* was published. It did not appear until 1624, fifteen years after he had left Virginia.

14. Counseil for Virginia, *A True Declaration of the Estate of the Colonie in Virginia, With a Confutation of Such Scandalous Reports as have Tended to the Disgrace of so Worthy an Enterprise* (London, 1610). See the "Virtual Jamestown Archive" at http://etext.lib.virginia.edu/etcbin/jamestown-browse?id=J1059 (last accessed 26 March 2006).

15. See Gallagher, et al., *Literature of Justification: Jamestown*, at http://digital.lib.lehigh.edu/trial/justification/jamestown/essay/1/.

are worse than those beasts which are of most wilde and savage nature.[16]

This early development of an english narrative to rationalize the occupation of Virginia gave new impetus to european imaginations about human primal beginnings, which were increasingly described in terms of the english and european imaginations about America and its Native Peoples. By the mid-seventeenth century, in his *Leviathan* Thomas Hobbes builds his notion of an original, primeval state of human beings as totally given over to "warre" and violence, "the war of every man against every man," perpetuating the White lie about indigenous peoples. People lived in "continual fear and danger of violent death," with the result, claimed Hobbes, that peoples' lives were "solitary, poor, nasty, brutish and short." Hobbes evidentiary warrant for his description of the primal human state is vested in using America, sight unseen, as an example, that "savage people in many places in America" continued to live in this primeval state of violence. Here Hobbes is already romanticizing english civilization as a superior state of being to the savagery of those still closer to the primal state.

Later in the same century, John Locke, again never having been to America but financially invested himself in the Carolina Company, continued the developing english narrative in ways that depreciate the value of indigenous peoples in north America. The inadequacies are particularly apparent to him in his discussion of property in the *Second Treatise*. Indian people are lacking in Locke's mind because they are unable to generate greater wealth from their property. Namely, their property is unimproved, and Locke's fundamental doctrine for the making of private property has to do with labor expelled to improve land and ultimately to justify the english ownership of Indian land.

> There cannot be a clearer demonstration of any thing, than several nations of the Americans are of this, who are rich in land, and poor in all the comforts of life; whom nature having furnished as liberally as any other people, with the materials of plenty, i.e. a fruitful soil, apt to produce in abundance, what might serve for food, raiment, and delight; yet for want of improving it by labour, have not one hundredth part of the conveniencies we enjoy: and a king of

16. Manahan, "Robert Gray's *A Goodspeed to Virginia*," at http://digital.lib.lehigh.edu/trial/justification/jamestown/essay/4/.

a large and fruitful territory there, feeds, lodges, and is clad worse
than a day-labourer in England.[17]

This narrative defining the uncivilized barbarism of Indian peoples continues through american history actually into the present, continuing
to show up in technical textbooks and just as frequently in newspaper
editorializing.

## COLONIZATION OF THE MIND—
## AND THE WORK OF CHRISTIAN MISSIONS

As the colonizer romanticizes the Self and demonizes the Other, the
colonizer must also pay attention to a perceived need to transform the
colonized into a sort of copy of the colonizer's self.[18] At some point, colonization moves beyond military conquest and the exercise of political and
economic subjection over the colonized Other. As many post-colonial
writers have noted, the forced transformation of the minds of the colonized becomes an important part of the process of subjection. Europeans
in America were convinced that they lived a civilized life; Natives were
unequivocally uncivilized. And this distinction certainly extended from
the beginnings of colonization in the Americas to the colonizers' sense
of the superiority of their religious convictions. In this part of my paper
I argue that missionary outreach to indigenous peoples by euro-western
missionaries always was and is a significant part of the process some indigenous writers have called the colonization of the mind. Since American
Indian peoples do not have "religion" *per se*,[19] the colonial imposition of

---

17. John Locke, *Second Treatise on Government*, V:41.

18. For Homi Bhabha, the colonized can be and must strive to be "almost the
same, but not white." See Bhabha, "Of Mimicry and Man." *October* 28 (Spring 1984)
126. Commenting on Bhabha, Anne McClintock, *Imperial Leather: Race, Gender and
Sexuality in the Colonial Contest* (New York: Routledge, 1995) 62, writes: "In Bhabha's
schema, mimicry is a flawed identity imposed on colonized people who are obliged to
mirror back an image of the colonials but in imperfect form."

19. Religion is one of those categories of cognition that seem so natural to White
amer-europeans that it is taken as a universal that applies to all peoples. American Indian
folk do not, however, divide the world up into sacred and secular. Hence all of life has its
religious intonations, which means that Indian folk are paying attention to their relationships with the spiritual at all times in everything that we do. See my entry, "Religion," in
*The Encyclopedia of the North American Indian*, ed. Frederick E. Hoxie (Boston: Houghton
Mifflin, 1996) 537–41. Most American Indian traditional people have characteristically
denied that their people ever had or engaged in any religion at all. Rather, these spokes-

Christianity (which was virtual U.S. Government policy, especially from the 1880s on[20]) represents an earthshaking, yet coerced, cultural shift in Indian community structures and in the value system that guides people's lives. Far from being an unmitigated good in Indian communities, it is part and parcel of the terrible poverty and the suffocating negative social statistics that characterize the Indian world today. Christianization began the process of colonizing Indian minds and attempting to force a shift in the indigenous worldview.

Indeed it was a clash of worldviews, but it was a clash that was long in the making. Robert Williams has demonstrated that the euro-western legal tradition that created the oppressive structures of "federal Indian law" in the U.S. has deep roots in medieval Christianity and christian legal discourses beginning wtih cannon law.[21] So a worldview of european (White) superiority is deeply rooted in the ontology and habitual thought patterns of all european peoples, perhaps most especially among those in the U.S. The result has been a colonizer romanicization of the Self's worldview and religious conviction as normative and universal, which in turn becomes a rationale for the missiological endeavor.

If the colonized have suffered the colonization of their minds, it should be stressed that the colonizer (including all varieties of christian

---

people would insist that their whole culture and social structure was and is infused with a spirituality that can not be separated from the rest of the community's life at any point. Green Corn Ceremony, Snake Dance, Kachinas, Sun Dance, sweat lodge ceremonies, and the pipe are not the religions of various tribes but rather these are specific ceremonial aspects of a world that includes countless ceremonies in any given tribal context, ceremonies performed by whole communities, clans, families or individuals on a daily, periodic, seasonal or occasional basis. While outsiders may identify a single main ceremony as the "religion" of a particular people, those people will likely see that ceremony as merely one extension of their day-to-day existence, all of which is experienced within ceremonial parameters and should be seen as "religious," but not as religion.

20. Note the U.S. Government role—along with protestant church leaders—in the Lake Mohonk Conferences of Friends of the Indian where the actual late nineteenth century strategy for "civilizing" the American Indian was crafted. See Tinker, "Tracing a Contour of Colonialism: American Indians and the Trajectory of Educational Imperialism," in Ward Churchill, *Kill the Indian, Save the Man: The Genocidal Impact of American Indian Residential Schools* (San Francisco: City Lights, 2004) xiii–xli. Also note Francis P. Prucha, *Americanizing the American Indians: Writing by the "Friends of the Indian," 1880–1900* (Lincoln: University of Nebraska Press, 1973), for excerpts from actual papers and presentations at the Lake Mohonk Conferences.

21. See Robert A. Williams Jr., *The American Indian in Western Legal Thought: The Discourses of Conquest* (Oxford: Oxford University Press, 1990).

missionaries) have also had their minds deeply impregnated with thought patterns, beliefs, ways of thinking and problem-solving that hold euro-western (and christian) peoples captive just as readily as the colonized are held captive. After centuries of shaping their interpretation of their Scriptures, eurowestern folk are boxed into particular ways of reading their own Bible and interpreting its stories and imperatives. While the process of imposing Christianity on the colonized has been tragic for countless communities of colonized peoples, the process has ultimately been just as tragic for those who believe they have been faithfully following the dictates of their "savior."

Christian missionaries and their theological languaging very quickly became a deeply ingrained part of the colonial systemic whole. And because the colonial project is never a clearly defined systematic process, it was easy enough for various colonialist players, perhaps especially including missionaries, to lose sight of the nefarious logic for colonizing Native minds that lay behind their own discourse and motivations. Thus, they continued (and continue) to participate in the process even in their naïveté. Indeed we could argue that much of euro-christian doctrinal language is rooted in some cultural past that has permeated the euro-christian colonial present. It has become such a permanent fixture in euro-christian discourse that it seems a perfectly natural part of the religious/theological whole. Yet christian doctrines, like the categories of race, gender, class and culture generally, are social constructions. As such they are much dependent on and influenced by the cultural milieu of the theologian and the social whole in which the theologian lives.

All too often there is a tendency in the development of christian theology to see the past, especially the distant past of the "early church," as somehow a pristine expression of the christian gospel without remembering that the colonizing process had already begun in that distant past of the history of early Christianity as Christianity moved from a jewish worldview to one that was given over to greek languaging and categories of cognition. This, too, is a romanticizing of history. And yet today the theological discourse of the early church gets adopted as a given in interpreting the biblical texts themselves and is usually imposed on the colonized Other without much thought as to questions of cultural appropriateness.

Yet, we dare not see Christianity as merely a set of normative doctrinal teachings that are somehow unaffected by the larger culture in which the religion thrives. Namely, we dare not presume that Christianity maintains some pure linguistic attachment to first century Palestine or even the fourth century of Nicea, etc. Rather, we know full well that early Christianity was shaped linguistically by its collision and collusion with Greek philosophy just as it continues to be affected by contemporary cultures. It was after all Greek philosophy that introduced the notion of substance into the early creation of and formulation of christian trinitarian thinking.[22] Of course, I have in mind here the third century (largely Greek) debate whether the "son" was of the same substance (*homoousios*) or merely a similar substance (*homooisias*) as the "father" in the early trinitarian formulation. Jewish language of Jesus's own day seems to have had no interest at all in talking about the divine as substance, something that is a purely platonic and post-platonic discussion. Any American Indian traditional thinker, for instance, would find the whole discussion about divine substance absolutely baffling, since all tribal traditions know of what amer-europeans call the divine only in terms of spirit. Spirit, they will say, is antithetical to matter or substance. And all spirit, ultimately, is the same spirit. The cultural prominence of the language of substance, however, forced early christian theologians / thinkers / writers to take the question of substance seriously even if the thought had not even occurred to the earliest palestinian (jewish) Christians. The point is that the language of the day, the particularity of the questions raised in the social whole, especially by those thinkers that are foundational for the social whole of their day, always affects public discourse and necessarily affects how people language their faith and, in turn, how they experience and ultimately live their faith.

By the time the english *invasion* began in Virginia (sorry for the choice of language here, but that is the Indian perspective[23]), the languaging of Christianity had been deeply affected by european philosophical discourse, whether it affirmed the whole of that discourse or not. Particularly, the questions raised by that discourse became questions

22. The language was influenced primarily by aristotelean materialism, even though the reigning philosophies of the Mediterranean of the early church period were some form of platonism: the middle- or neo-platonism of those days).

23. Note the title of the important volume on early english colonial history in America published more than three decades ago by Francis Jennings, *The Invasion of America: Indians, Colonialism, and the Cant of Conquest* (New York: Norton, 1976). Jennings is the former Director of the Newberry Library's D'Arcy McNickle Center for American Indian History.

necessarily embraced by people of faith and their key spokespeople (e.g., theologians). Then this culturally specific language gets imposed on other worlds willy nilly as if it were the gospel or some culturally neutral divine truth. The problematic here for American Indian cultures is that the Greek reified notion of deity is presumptively imposed on communities where, the concept that the missionaries identified with their own god, defies any move towards reification. The end result is the total loss, in many communities, of the very sophisticated indigenous notion of *wakonda* in favor of the imposition of the euro-cultural notion of a reified deity that stems not from the christian Bible but from the fourth century world of greek society.

Ultimately, the cultural knowledges about *wakonda* that Indian communities had and continue to have in many places in north America seem to be incompatible with euro-western christian theological notions of salvation. Cultural differences abound from Indian commitments to communitarian sensitivity and euro-western commitments to radical in-dividualism (crucial in the euro-christian salvation schema); to American Indian privileging of spatiality over temporality colliding with the funda-mental temporality of euro-western cultures and the ways that temporal-ity is constructed into euro-christian theologizing. I have often argued in the classroom that the first euro-western missionary to enter any indig-enous community immediately introduced division into that community with devastating effect. That these missionaries saw themselves from the beginning as working to replace Indian culture and values with their own is neither here nor there, actually. That was the effect in any case, the de-struction of Native cultures and value systems.

The colonization of the mind changes how one thinks about every-thing from religion to running tribal governments. Colonization of the mind is the ultimate genocide and the ultimate tragedy for indigenous peoples. Conversion means, finally, leaving behind this intimate sense of community wholeness and balance in favor of one's own (individual) spiritual security and salvation. It means surrendering all expectation and hope for a spatially oriented sense of balance and harmony in favor of temporal euro-christian eschatological expectations.

How will modern christians develop missiologies that are more ap-propriate to the values of the gospel and also appropriate to the pres-ent context of religious and cultural diversity in the U.S.? Indeed is any missiological project viable today? Given the disastrous history of euro-western mission practices—to the cultures and the peoplehood of those missionized—it would seem that there are no missioloigical projects that we might conceive that would have legitimacy of any kind. At least it must be argued that any time the powerful of the world (e.g., euro-western churches or mission organizations) attempt to convert the less powerful there are inherent problems involved that make the endeavor invariably a colonizing project that would make Jesus blush—with embarrassment and probably with the same anger he showed the money changers in the temple. There are the lingering problems of privileging and the universal sense of normativity that comes with certain kinds of privileging. By privileging I mean to point to the long eurowestern and particularly amer-european christian certainty of its own universality and, hence, superiority to other cultures and other religious traditions. The privileging of Whiteness is necessarily part of this notion of euro-christian universality, and ultimately gendered notions of male privileging need to be addressed in this context as well. Indeed, the eurowestern christian narrative has postured itself as normative and universal, the only access to salvation, almost from the fourth century on (marked by the so-called conversion of Constantine, ca. 323).

On the other hand, another kind of missiological project might yet prove to be legitimate and a much closer reflection of the New Testament gospel sense of mission. Namely, as I have argued in another essay, perhaps it is time for christian people to stop preaching Jesus and to simply BE Jesus, that is, to reflect Jesus, Jesus's values, Jesus's teachings, Jesus's own attitudes in every minute of one's life. BE *agapē*, that is be that sort of love that intends the best for the other person, but intend it materially and physically and forget imposing one's own spirituality on the other as some superior way of existence.

Let me close simply by suggesting that romance would call on people merely to celebrate their successes (while concealing the failures). Tragedy, on the other hand, calls for confession and repentance—and only then is salvation a real possibility. The latter have been distinctly absent in White America's and christian missionaries' relationships with Native Peoples.

2

# A Failure to Communicate

## How Christian Missionary Assumptions Ignore Binary Patterns of Thinking within Native-American Communities

BARBARA ALICE MANN

*Nothing could be more remote from one another than the cultural bases of Native-American and European-Christian thought, yet for four centuries, mistaken missionary chronicles have been allowed to mis/represent true Native philosophies. Christian cultures operate from a base number of One, whereas Native-American cultures operate from a base number of Two. This disparity especially makes Christian and Native spiritualities mutually incomprehensible. Commonplace Christian One-thinking anticipates ones—one God, one life, one spouse, one "truth," etc.—whereas Native Two-Thinking expects binaries—an interactive Sky-Earth cosmos, reincarnation, multiple spouses, blended "truths," etc. One-Thinking emphasizes Manichean dichotomies that set up enmity: two of anything implies that one is an impostor or a challenger to be defeated. Meantime, Two-Thinking requires collaboration, seeing one of anything as necessarily incomplete. Colonialism resulted in the imposition of many Christian ideas (e.g., God as solitary Creator) on Native cultures, but many Natives are now attempting to deChristianize their thinking, reclaiming the traditional system of binaries as the appropriate structure of reality.*

## SETTING THE STAGE: HISTORICAL CONSIDERATIONS

When the fact of the Americas first entered European consciousness, it came as a massive culture shock. Here, completely unaccounted for in the Christian Bible was an entire hemisphere full of continents, filled with millions of people living happily organized, well-fed, disease-free, l-o-n-g lives without ever once having heard of Jesus. If the Bible were truly the "word of God," then somehow, God seemed to have been left out of the geographical loop. The Church sought to salve its PSTDD (Post-Traumatic Discovery Disorder) by missionizing, a form of denial that sought to dissolve the Christian conundrum by forcing Natives into line with its pre-existing explanation of cosmic purpose.

Contact was just as shattering on the Native side, not because our cultures rejected the sheer idea of Europe, but because Europeans behaved in nakedly aggressive ways, for which nothing in our cultural basket of expectations had prepared us. Establishing peace through gifting was the first tack we took with any new actors on the block. The proper response to gifting was for the recipient to return with larger gifts. Constant warfare, in the form of invasion, dispossession, enslavement, and forced assimilation, was simply not a legitimate response to gifting, so that settlers' unremitting, scorched-earth hostilities—whose advance guard was almost always the Christian mission—left us flat-footed in shock.

From the get-go, then, neither side had a clue as to what the other side was doing, although each cheerfully assumed the other side had a perfect grasp of its operative paradigm. This continued until Native systems were crushed in favor of European systems politically, socially, and economically, but nowhere was it more damaging to real communication than in the spiritual realm. For both sides, spiritual philosophy underpinned all the rest, so that dislocation here disrupted everything else.

Much of the antique and on-going misunderstanding of Native American spiritualities comes to the present courtesy of either missionary mistakes or later academic exaltation of Native "prophets" such as *Tenskwatawa* of the Shawnees or *Neolin* of the Lenapes, who were really more the product of Euro-Christian promotion than of Native acceptance. Missionaries on the ground with these "prophets" found their philosophies important enough to emphasize in their chronicles, because the ideas the "prophets" were spouting were sufficiently Christianized to look like spiritual competition with Christianity.

Take, for instance, *Sganyadaiyoh* ("Handsome Lake") of my people, the Senecas. His 1799 *Gaiwiiyo* (*Code of Handsome Lake*) was entirely cribbed from the Christian Bible, after his Quaker-educated cousin, Henry O'Bail, had read it aloud to him. Although he never accepted Christianity, O'Bail was locked in a massive cultural struggle with his father, "Cornplanter" (*Shinnewannah, Hosanowanna*). To survive invasion and conquest, the son wanted to modernize—i.e., assimilate European cultural values—whereas the father insisted upon conserving traditional culture. Reading and translating the Bible to *Sganyadaiyoh* was part of O'Bail's modernizing, whack-a-dad scheme.[1]

Missionizing always works best on the most marginalized members of the target group. In this case, both O'Bail and *Sganyadaiyoh* were vulnerable outcasts, although the attention granted O'Bail by the missionaries lent him some artificial importance. O'Bail's cousin-brother,[2] *Sganyadaiyoh* had started out as a man with prospects, having been elevated to the important position of *Sganyadaiyoh* (a position title, not a personal name) while he still looked as if he might have turned out to have been useful to the people. However, watching the total destruction of Iroquoia during the Revolution had completely undermined any hope that *Sganyadaiyoh* had entertained for cultural survival. By 1799, he was crushed, a man broken in every possible way.[3]

By 1799, neither man was respected by the traditional Senecas. In particular, *Sganyadaiyoh* was a hopeless drunk, an embarrassment both to his family and to those who had put him in office. Shortly after O'Bail had,

1. C. M. Barbeau, *Huron and Wyandot Mythology*, Anthropological Series, 11 Memoir 80 (Ottawa: Government Printing Bureau, 1915) 22; Anthony F. C. Wallace, *The Death and Rebirth of the Senecas* (New York: Knopf, 1970) 188, 245, 330, 333; Arthur C. Parker, *The Code of Handsome Lake, the Seneca Prophet*, New York State Museum Bulletin 163, Education Department Bulletin, no. 530 (Albany: State University of New York Press, 1913), 11; Arthur C. Parker, "Notes on the Ancestry of Cornplanter," *Researches and Transactions of the New York State Archaeological Association*, Lewis H. Morgan Chapter (1927, reprint; New York: Times Presses, 1970). For my smooth treatment of the O'Bail-*Sganyadaiyoh* interface, see Barbara Alice Mann, *Iroquoian Women: The Gantowisas* (New York: Peter Lang, 2000) 315–16.

2. Although O'Bail and *Sganyadaiyoh* shared a common father, they were, by Iroquoian count, cousins. Many western texts list the pair as brothers, however. Lewis Henry Morgan, *The League of the Haudenosaunee, or Iroquois*, 2 vols. (1851; New York: Franklin, 1901) 1:218.

3. Bruce Elliott Johansen and Barbara Alice Mann, eds., *Encyclopedia of the Haudenosaunee (Iroquois League)* (Westport, CN: Greenwood, 2000) 145–51.

Christianly enough, taken him to a mountaintop to translate the Bible to him, *Sganyadaiyoh* began his series of visions, all of which aped the old Christian script by raising him up from the depths to salvation.[4] Noting what looked like *Sganyadaiyoh's* temperance message, both Thomas Jefferson and the Society of Friends (to which Jefferson's administration had handed governance of the Iroquoian reservations) promoted *Sganyadaiyoh* as a leader in the settler struggle to keep alcohol out of Native hands.[5] It was by cooperating with prohibition that *Sganyadaiyoh* eventually rose to the position of land negotiator with the settlers, but since he was really the U.S. government's man, he was never very successful in protecting Seneca lands from seizure.[6]

The fact that his *Gaiwiiyo* echoed Christian concepts largely went unnoticed by either Church or academic scholars until the turn of the twenty-first century, but not because Natives did not question it. I recall how shocked I was to learn that Anthony Wallace's *Death and Rebirth of the Seneca* (1970) was hailed in academia for its ground-breaking grasp of Iroquoian thought, when, in fact, all it did was promote *Sganyadaiyoh's* abject Christianizations as Real Seneca Philosophy. In fact, had *Sganyadaiyoh* not had the backing of U.S. church and state, he would never have gotten anywhere with his totally non-traditional *Gaiwiiyo*. In Ohio, where League peoples still formed a vigorous front against invasion and land seizure until the 1820s, *Sganyadaiyoh* was impatiently rejected as an impostor and, with his infamous "witch hunts," a murderer of the worst sort, of helpless elder women. To this day, no traditional Ohio Iroquois listen to his words.

Indeed, until 1848, when the U.S. Government completely stripped the traditional Iroquoian Clan Mothers and Chiefs of their power, imposing instead a U.S.-friendly "government" on Iroquoia, *Sganyadaiyoh* was scorned in New York, too, seen as a poor excuse for a prophet who

---

4. See my discussion of the Christianizations of the *Gaiwiiyo* in Mann, *Iroquoian Women*, 316.

5. Parker, *Code of Handsome Lake*, 10.

6. Anthony F. C. Wallace, *Jefferson and the Indians: The Tragic Fate of the First Americans* (Cambridge, Mass.: Belknap Press of Harvard University Press, 1999) 291; National Archives, *Secretary of War, Letters Sent*, 1800–1824, Vol. A, 183–87; National Archives, *Secretary of War, Letters Sent*, 1800–1824, Vol. A, 183–87, 194–95; Thomas Jefferson, *Writings* (New York: Library of America, 1984) 555–57.

admitted to forgetting some of his visions and withholding others.[7] His death-squad attacks on opponents, especially Clan Mothers, had earned him the undying hatred of the longhairs, who correctly charged him with destroying traditional culture. Even as late as the turn of the twentieth century, two-thirds of the New York Iroquois rejected the *Gaiwiiyo*, one third because they had become Christian and the other third because they remained loyal to the old traditional stories, found in neither Christianity nor the *Gaiwiiyo*. Nevertheless, anthropologists, and through them historians, promptly decided that *Sganyadaiyoh's* Longhouse Religion was THE REAL LIVE IROQUOIAN RELIGION, so that today, it is almost impossible to challenge that mistake in academic circles.

New Agers are also ignorant and destructive of Native traditional content, largely because they are lapsed Christians, still (if unconsciously) working from the Christian paradigms industriously seeded into descriptions of Native culture by the missionaries. For instance, chroniclers assumed that the "Great Spirit," "Master of Life," or "Grandfather God" were somehow *real* Native American terms, instead of Euro-Christian interpolations. In fact, Natives have no high-God concept, let alone God concepts that mimic male-dominated hierarchies. Instead, we have Councils of Elder Spirits operating in replication of our participatory democracies, while almost all of our heads of cosmic households are female, for instance, *Aetensic* of the Iroquois, *Kokomthena* of the Shawnees, White Buffalo Calf Woman of the Lakotas, Spider Old Woman of the Hopis, and Raven of the Haidas.

Unfortunately, Christian missionaries, academics, and bureaucrats continue to impose "Creator" talk on us, as did, for example, the Senate Joint Resolution of the 108th U.S. Congress (Second Session, Calendar 638) on July 15, 2004. Native cultures had a "deep and abiding belief in the Creator," it declared, thereby promoting one of the most obdurately flawed

---

7. For U.S.-imposed government, see Diane Rothenberg, "Erosion of Power: An Economic Basis for the Selective Conservatism of Seneca Women in the Nineteenth Century," *Western Canadian Journal of Anthropology* 6:3 (1978) 116–17. An 1868 revision strengthened the disempowerment of women, Diane Rothenberg, "The Mothers of the Nations: Seneca Resistance to Quaker Intervention," in *Women and Colonization*, ed. Mona Etienne and Eleanor Burke Leacock (New York: Praeger, 1980) 68. For ridicule at *Sganyadaiyoh's* having forgotten visions, see Wallace, *Death and Rebirth*, 290, and Arthur C. Parker, *The Life of Ely S. Parker: Last Grand Sachem of the Iroquois and General Grant's Military Secretary* (Buffalo: Buffalo Historical Society, 1919) 325. For withholding visions, see Parker, *Code of Handsome Lake*, 12.

propositions on record about Native philosophy. Traditionally, there is no solitary, omnipotent, goal-oriented "Creator." First, the spirits are not *all-powerful*; each simply knows more about itself and its immediate purview than does anyone else. Second, Native stories typically feature *accident* as the precipitating cause of creation. Third, creation is a *joint project* of all the spirits of Earth and Sky acting in concert. (More traditional terms for Earth and Sky are Blood and Breath, respectively, in the woodlands, and, west of the Mississippi River, Water and Air, respectively.)

For example, the Iroquoian creation story starts with the Sky People passing by a no-account, podunk little water planet one day, where their Elder Spirits wound up the inadvertent hosts of an impromptu council, as the Elder Spirits of that water planet, Earth, seized the opportunity to suggest that land life be created on it. The Elder Sky Spirits (of whom the individual actors among the Sky People were not even necessarily aware) had no particular objection to the Earth-forming plan. For their part, the Elder Earth Spirits very much wanted creation to happen. Consequently, a consensus was reached by the Elder Spirits of both Sky and Earth to begin land life on Earth.[8]

Then, time passed.

Next comes the story of *Aetensic*, The Sky Woman, Grandmother. After a series of events, Sky Woman accidentally falls to Earth, inciting the physical creation of Turtle Island by the water animals already extant. After Turtle offers her carapace, and the animals smear a little dirt from the ocean's floor over it, Sky Woman begins to walk. With each step, the land spreads far and wide. Next, Turtle Island is filled with crops invented by The Lynx, the daughter of Sky Woman. The quadruplets, two boys and two girls born to The Lynx, complete creation.[9] None of the actors in the First Family is particularly aware of being part of a larger plan; each is just struggling to survive, day-by-day.

All the traditional paradigms are exposed in this story. In addition to its multiple, unconscious actors moving through crisis by accident and the social concepts it models, this story posits the central social relation-

---

8. Harriet Maxwell Converse [*Yaiewanoh*], *Myths and Legends of the New York State Iroquois*, ed. Arthur C. Parker, New York State Museum Bulletin 125, Education Department Bulletin No. 437 (Albany: State University of New York Press, 1908) 31, 33.

9. Johansen and Mann, *Encyclopedia of the Haudenosaunee*, 87–95. Later anthropologists seeded the notion of the Great Turtle as male, but in the original stories, earth is *always* female.

ship as the mother-daughter bond, with the secondary relationship being the sister-brother bond. Just as crucially, when the Iroquois allude to The One Good Mind of the creation story, they are talking about the *consensus council* of the Elder Spirits of Sky and Earth, who came to be of One Mind concerning the proposition that land life be created on Earth. Under such a schema, "The Bad Mind" simply means a *lack of consensus.* The terms "Good Mind" and "Bad Mind," then, have nothing whatsoever to do with Christian ideas of God and the Devil, as is mistakenly asserted on a regular basis.

The sacred stories of Sky Woman and her Daughter, the great creators of Turtle Island, were so threatening to the early Catholic missionaries, that they "fixed" what they saw as flaws inherent in them. For instance, to fix the problem of too many female actors, missionaries promoted the decidedly tertiary story cycle of the male Twins of the Iroquoian Creation Epoch, completely dropping the contrapuntal female Twins.[10] Not yet satisfied, the missionaries also wrote the quadruplets' mother, The Lynx, out of the story. They could not quite excise Grandmother, *Aetensic*, the Sky Woman, from the story, so they depicted her as *evil.*

Ultimately, after four hundred years' worth of focus on the *important* part of the Creation story—the male Twins—successive missionaries had completely transmuted the elder twin into God and the younger, into the Devil. In 1632, the Franciscan missionary Gabriel Sagard did briefly wonder how God had wound up with a grandmother, but the churchmen simply ignored that problem until it went away.[11] When Cornplanter tried to reinstate the traditional stories in 1827, the Quakers wrote off his recital as the mental meanderings of a senile old man.[12]

Turning the Iroquoian Creator both solitary and male was no isolated instance. Using old missionary records, nineteenth- and twentieth-century anthropologists regularly parsed female creators until they somehow turned spouselessly male. In the 1940s, anthropologists Charles and Erminie Voegelin declared the Shawnee creator to be male, despite clear evidence that *Kokomthena* was female. Similarly, *Selu*, the Corn Mother

10. J. N. B. Hewitt, "Iroquoian Cosmology, Second Part," in *Forty-third Annual Report of the Bureau of American Ethnology to the Secretary of the Smithsonian Institution, 1925–1926* (Washington, DC: Government Printing Office, 1928) 468.

11. Gabriel Sagard, *The Long Journey to the Country of the Hurons,* ed. George M. Wong, trans. H. H. Langton (1632, reprint; Toronto: Chaplain Society, 1939) 169.

12. Parker, "Notes on the Ancestry of Cornplanter," 17–20.

of the Cherokees, was disenfranchised in favor of her husband, *Kanati*, originally the Lucky Hunter, who transmuted into the current Cherokee, male "Creator," heavily modeled on Christianity.[13] Anthropologists thereafter presented the old missionary interpolations as Real Indian Creation Myths, instead of what they were, evangelical restructurings of traditional stories later picked up and passed along by anthropologists.

These sorts of distortion went unchallenged for a very long time, not in small measure because, under U.S. law, it was illegal for Natives to practice their own spiritualities until 1978, when the Native American Religious Freedom Act graciously gave Natives the same freedom of religion Constitutionally guaranteed to all other American citizens. Unfortunately, many who grew up under the governmental, missionary-run Boarding School system had been taught nothing but the doctrines of whatever Christian sect had controlled their school. Those Natives interested in cultural recovery perforce looked to western "primary" sources, only to find "The Great Spirit" in them and assume that he must have been traditional, after all.

Just barely discernible in western sources are the truly Native ideas that:

- assume the cosmos consists of binary units

- stress the matrilineage of the cosmos as well as of peoples

- speak of creation as a collaborative effort, including both females and males

- view spirits and humans as about equally powerful, within their respective spheres of influence

- lack moral dualism

## CONFLICTING PARADIGMS

The difficulty here is really one of conflicting paradigms, as symbolized by the base numbers of western, as opposed to Native, culture.[14] The base number of Christian European culture is ONE, showing up in such

13. Barbara Alice Mann, "'Where Are Your Women?' Missing in Action," in *Unlearning the Language of Conquest,* ed. Don Trent Jacobs (Austin: University of Texas Press, 2006) 125.

14. I canvass this concept in great detail in chapter 4 of Barbara Alice Mann, *Native Americans, Archaeologists, and the Mounds* (New York: Peter Lang, 2003) 169–238.

propositions as the *one* god with the *one* son, who gave *one* soul to everyone living her *one* life in pursuit of her *one* true love. In the West, two of anything instinctively pulls up the Manichean Dichotomy, under whose rubrics, two of anything means that one must be an impostor to be driven out in favor of the One Right and True Thing. I call this paradigm ONE-THINKING, and it is so pervasive in popular Euro-American culture that the entertainment industry needs but to tap its mythology to chill and thrill the audience. For instance, the popular, cult movie and TV series, *The Highlander*, successfully used, "There can be only one!" as its tagline, but the maxim stood out to me because my reaction was one of bewilderment. I still do not quite understand the logic of its premise.

By contrast, Two is the base number of Native America. ONE cannot exist unless it is as a unit consisting of Two matched halves. This is why the Iroquoian Twins of East and West, abstracted by the old missionaries as God and the Devil, cannot possibly be a Native construct. The Twins *collaborate* to create one unit, the Iroquoian Direction of the Sky; they can not compete against one another yet still achieve this collaboration. It is only as two working as one that they can hold up the East–West path that Brother Sun runs daily through the Sky.

A solitary Direction of the Sky necessarily results in imbalance, however, and on many levels. First, the East–West path needs a countervailing North–South path. Second, as a unit, the male Brother Sun needs a counterpart female orb. In other words, the halved East–West whole of the Direction of the Sky now forms one unit that needs to be fully replicated by a countervailing twin unit. Enter the other half of the quadruplets in the original Iroquoian creation story.

This second halved whole is completed by the female twins of North and South, the pair entirely slighted by the missionaries in canvassing Iroquoian creation. North–South is represented by the path of Grandmother Moon, who, once every generation (18.61 years), runs The Split Sky of the North-South axis during what westerners call "the standstill of the moon." With the North–South axis, we now have a cross, which looks something like a plus sign ╫, a unit of Two constructed by Four. Typically, the horizontal bar (↔) is seen as representing the East–West axis (E↔W), whereas the vertical bar (↕) stands for the North–South axis ($^N$↕$_S$), resulting in the cross ╫. This is what I call TWO-BY-FOUR THINKING, as shown below, in Figure 1.

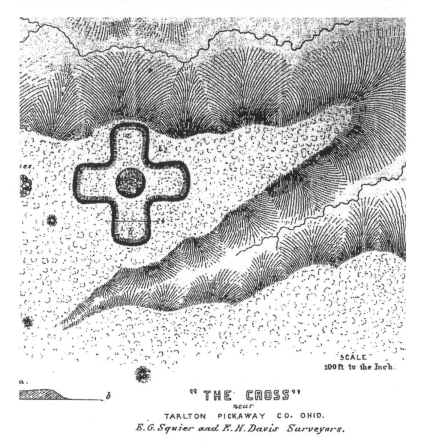

FIGURE 1: The Plus-Sign "Cross" Mound, shows one variation of the Earth-Sky motif. SOURCE: Ephraim George Squier and E. H. Davis, *Ancient Monuments of the Mississippi Valley: Comprising the Results of Extensive Original Surveys and Explorations*, Smithsonian Contributions to Knowledge, 2 vols. (1848, reprint; New York: Johnson Reprint Corporation, 1965) 1:98, facing.

Figure 1, the Plus-Sign "Cross" Mound, shows a mound schematic demonstrating plus-sign iconography in action. Of course, this motif greatly excited some of the first Christians who saw it. Their explanation included a visit from Jesus before he left the earthly plane, but in fact, the mound shows the plus-sign concept of the cardinal directions, one of the most common motifs in Native North America. On the ground, they are the Four Mothers, often represented by Horned Serpents; in the air, they are the Four Winds, often Cloudland Eagles. The Serpent-Eagle is a common Native pairing, iconographic of binary thought.

Plus-sign iconography is more complex than simple compass points, however. Typically, Native America cocks the cardinal points, rotating them to the Northwest and Southeast, into the configuration shown below, as Figure 2, The Two-by-Four of the Cardinal Directions. In Figure 2, the Iroquoian $^N\updownarrow_S$ female pair includes the Blue Lynx of the North, referencing blue glacial ice, and the Sweet Woman of the South, referencing yellow corn. The E↔W male pair includes Sapling, the red-dawn Strawberry Man, juxtaposed by his sibling, black Flint, the Humpbacked Runner of the Western Rim. In the E↔W pair, the sweetness of strawberries matches the sharpness of flint (a cutting tool), just as the sweetness of corn matches the sharpness of cold in the $^N\updownarrow_S$ pair. Each half heightens the impact of its complement.

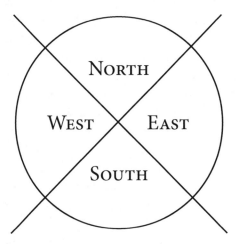

**FIGURE 2:** The Two-by-Four of the Cardinal Directions, shows the traditional, tilted concept of the Twinned Direction of the male Sky (E↔W) and female Split Sky (N$\updownarrow$S). Figure created by Barbara Mann.

Not only do the East–West/male and North–South/female pairs balance one another, but a second set of units also exists as the cross-pairs of $^N\updownarrow_W$ and S↔E. North and West are seen as wrinkled units (where danger lurks), balancing South and East, the smooth units (where comfort resides). The blue of the North and the black (traditionally, a deep blue-purple) of the West are equated with invisibility, difficulty, and death. The red East and yellow South are connected with success, nutrition, and life. Both wrinkled and smooth are good and, as it happens, necessary to life. Another handy way of referencing these cosmic binaries is through gender and age. Male is Sky/Age, while its female complement is Earth/ Youth. (Sky means outer space, not the blue atmosphere. Sky existed before Earth hosted life; hence, Earth is younger.)

Native Two-THINKING requires ideas quite foreign to Euro-Christian ONE-THINKING. For instance, Two-THINKING not only takes reincarnation for granted, but also just assumes that every human (a single unit) must be composed of *two* spiritual halves, evident as a Blood/Water/Earth spirit and a Breath/Air/Sky spirit.[15] Marriage is the active replication of the cosmic two-by-four, combining two units (male/female people), each composed of its own two halves (the Earth/Sky spirit combo), into the halved whole, ultimately recreating the concept in Figure 2.

The Sky spirit transmits through the breath of the father and lives in the brain, regulating ethical and intellectual concerns. The Earth spirit derives from the blood of the mother and lives, depending on the culture, in the marrow of the bones or in the gut. Its sphere of influence is passion and morality. *Both halves are necessary.* By itself, either runs amok. Sky alone is cleverness devoid of ethics. (Think Enron.) Earth alone is passion devoid of reasoning. (Think Jihad.) Anyone with just one spirit is in grave danger of criminal insanity, so that when the missionaries announced they had but one soul (spirit), it filled the people with fear of them.

People were very alert to where things fell "naturally" into the Earth or the Sky half of physical reality. Table 1 below, The Halved Cosmos, shows some of the things most commonly found in Earth and Sky halves of the physical cosmos. By and large, anything that lives in fields, including agriculture, all crops, towns, waterways, and families, are Earth and female. Conversely, anything lives in the forest, including trees, deer, mad bears (sasquatches), and mountains are Sky and male. Anything that flies through the air, like an arrow or an atlatl dart, is Sky and male. Anything that enters into the ground, like seeds or caves, is Earth and female. (One of the reasons bears are heavy medicine is because they live both in the forest and in caves, i.e., they are Boundary-Crossers of the first magni-

15. Reuben Gold Thwaites, ed. and trans., *The Jesuit Relations: Travels and Explorations of the Jesuit Missionaries in New France, 1610–1619*, 73 vols. (New York: Pageant, 1959) 10:287; Joseph François Lafitau, *Customs of the American Indians Compared with the Customs of Primitive Times*, ed. and trans. William N. Fenton and Elizabeth L. Moore, 2 vols. (1724, reprint; Toronto: Champlain Society, 1974) 1:230; Daniel G. Brinton, *The Myths of the New World: A Treatise on the Symbolism and Mythology of the Red Race of America* (1868, reprint; New York: Greenwood, 1969) 252–53.

tude.) Things dealing with conception and birth are Earth and female. Things dealing with war and death are Sky and male, showing the basic reasoning behind the rigorously enforced Native American law against rape.[16] Men conducting wars dared not mix the life medicine of female Earth (potential conception) with the war medicine of male Sky (potential casualties), because the life/Earth–death/Sky mixture was explosively likely to bounce back on the man, killing him and any male comrades around him.

## TABLE 1: THE HALVED COSMOS

| Blood / Water / Earth | Breath / Air / Sky |
|---|---|
| • Agriculture | • Hunting |
| • Turtle | • Wolf |
| • Youth | • Age |
| • Women | • Men |
| • Snake | • Eagle |
| • Square | • Circle |

TABLE 1: The Halved Cosmos, gives an example of how the complementary binaries work. Table created by Barbara Mann.

The clan halves (for the Iroquois, of Turtle/Earth and Wolf/Sky) were carefully constructed to echo Earth-Sky patterns. Each clan half hosted several lineal clans within itself. Moreover, people not only had to know the clan (Female/Earth–Male/Sky) halves, but also the national (Elder/Sky–Younger/Earth) half, to which they belonged. This gave everyone *two* identities: I am, for example, Bear Clan and Seneca Nation. To this day, people need to know not only their lineal birth clan, but also which clan *half* it falls into, because they must marry into the opposite half or commit incest. That is, all of the people in lineal clans of the Wolf (Sky) Half must seek mates from lineal clans within the Turtle (Earth) Half. Those who fail

16. Westerners are well aware of the no-rape policy. See Sally Roesch Wagner, "The Root of Oppression Is the Loss of Memory: The Iroquois and the Early Feminist Vision," in *Iroquois Women: An Anthology*, ed. William Guy Spittal (1988, reprint; Ohsweken, Ontario: Iroquois Publishing and Craft Supplies, Ltd., 1990) 225; Gregory Evans Dowd, *A Spirited Resistance: North American Indians Struggle for Unity, 1745–1815* (Baltimore: Johns Hopkins University Press, 1992) 9–11.

in this are ejected into the Eel Clan, which, dishonorably enough, belongs to neither cosmic half.

## NATIVE-AMERICAN WRITING SYSTEMS

Because Native American writing systems are conceptually so different from European writing systems, the settlers completely missed their existence, but writing systems also echoed the paired cosmos. For instance, *kipu* was a complicated system of the Incas, consisting of seventeen colored strings that made meaning according to two criteria: the colors being combined, and the points on the strings at which they were knotted together. The distribution and placement of knots by color could convey fairly sophisticated ideas, in this case, mostly mathematical.

In the eastern woodlands, wampum belts composed another binary writing system, this one through white and "black" (dark blue-purple) beads. A variety of characters could take on different meanings, depending upon which color the character was and its context on the belt. A diamond shape denoted a national council, for example. Whether it was black on white or white on black conveyed different takes on the idea. Like character writing everywhere, wampum could be read and understood by people from mutually unintelligible language groups, so that the Choctaws did not need to speak Seneca to read a Seneca message belt. Again, very sophisticated messages, in this case, linguistic, could be written into wampum. By the way, double wampum, or official messages, had two sides, Sky and Earth, each to have been read aloud by a team of Sky and Earth speakers.[17] The Sky speaker addressed the Earth (Turtle) half of the audience, whereas the Earth speaker address the Sky (Wolf) half of the audience.

Earth writing was necessarily more iconographic because making the ceremonial mounds was much more labor- and planning-intensive than knotting a wampum belt. Thus, a few symbols came to enjoy wide recognition as representing the cosmic interaction of Sky and Earth. There

---

17. J. N. B. Hewitt, "Wampum," in *Handbook of American Indians North of Mexico*, ed. Frederick Webb Hodge (New York: Rowman & Littlefield, 1965) 908; John Heckewelder, *History, Manners, and Customs of the Indian Nations Who Once Inhabited Pennsylvania and the Neighboring States*, The First American Frontier Series (1820, 1876, reprint; New York; Arno, 1971) 108; Barbara Mann, "The Fire at Onondaga: Wampum as Proto-Writing," *Akwesasne Notes*, 26th Anniversary Issue 1.1 (1995) 40–48.

were two sets of such symbols in the eastern woodlands, the circle-square complex and the nested circle design.

The most popular design in the Ohio valley involved the square ■ of Earth and the circle ● of Sky. These could be represented in multiple ways as a:

- square with a pathway connecting it to the circle
- square inside a circle
- a circle inside a plus sign

Figure 3, Square-and-Circle Motifs in Mound Writing, shows various circle-square possibilities. The largest complex shows a circle connected to a square via a pathway, the most common motif, by far. In the lower left-hand side is a square within a circle. A quick reference back to Figure 1 shows that the circle lies dead-center of the plus sign.

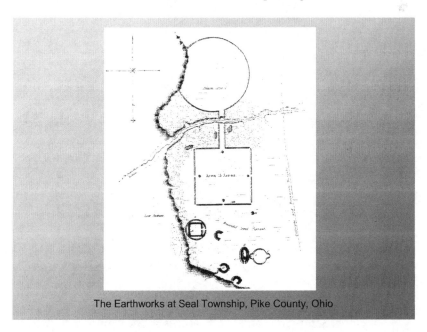

The Earthworks at Seal Township, Pike County, Ohio

**FIGURE 3:** Square-and-Circle Motifs in Mound Writing, shows how paired earth-writing was deployed. Notice the smaller motif including the Square of Earth within the Circle of Sky. SOURCE: Ephraim George Squier and E. H. Davis, *Ancient Monuments of the Mississippi Valley: Comprising the Results of Extensive Original Surveys and Explorations,* Smithsonian Contributions to Knowledge, 2 vols. (1848, reprint; New York: Johnson Reprint Corporation, 1965) 1:66, facing.

The other motifs, presaged in the right-hand bottom of Figure 3, Square-and-Circle Motifs in Mound Writing, bring us to the second set of iconic representations, nested circles. Although less common in the Ohio valley than the circle-square design, nested circles are very common in the lower Mississippi valley. Figure 4, below, Concentric and Dome Mound Motifs, demonstrates the underlying concept of the circular motif, which is based on the interaction of Earth (Turtle Island, or North America), in the form of the innermost circle, and Sky, in the form of the outermost circle. There are two possible vantage points, the profile and the overhead view. Seen in profile, the lower arch represents the turtle's back, or Earth, whereas the upper arch represents the Sky above. The overhead view of the same concept shows concentric circles, with the larger Sky surrounding the whole shell of the swimming turtle. These motifs are seen in Figures 5 and 6, below.

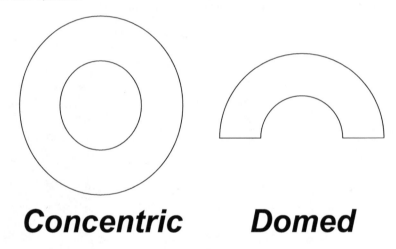

## *Concentric*     *Domed*

FIGURE 4: Concentric Mound and Domed Motifs, are based on Grandmother Turtle, who carries Turtle Island (North America) on her back. Figure created by Barbara Mann.

Figure 5, Semi-circle and Circle Motifs in the Mounds, shows both versions of the nested-circle motif. In the top, left-hand quadrant, there are a series of three semi-circles. Immediately below them are one large and three smaller nested circles. (Circles left an opening for ceremonially entering the nested full circles.) A wonderful Sky-writing noticed by the Iroquois was in the semi-circular pairs of the Pleiades and the

Cluster (Corona Borealis). For the Iroquois, midwinter is a women's time of year, properly heralded by the women's constellation of the Pleiades, visible directly overhead at midnight around the second week in January. Midsummer is a men's time of year, in this instance, announced by the men's constellation of The Cluster, visible overhead at midnight around the second week of July.

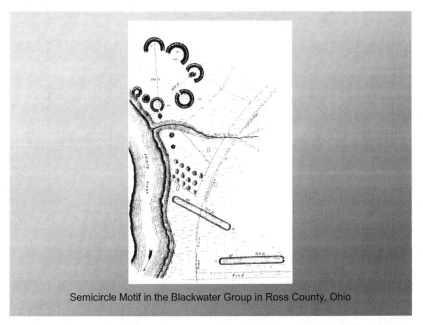

Semicircle Motif in the Blackwater Group in Ross County, Ohio

**FIGURE 5:** Semi-circle and Circle Motifs in the Mounds, shows both the profile of Earth and Sky as well as the overhead view of the same binaries. SOURCE: Ephraim George Squier and E. H. Davis, *Ancient Monuments of the Mississippi Valley: Comprising the Results of Extensive Original Surveys and Explorations*, Smithsonian Contributions to Knowledge, 2 vols. (1848, reprint; New York: Johnson Reprint, 1965) 1:61, facing.

These two constellations are shown in Figure 6, The Iroquoian Night Sky. Polaris marks the center of the Sky, dividing it into its male and female halves. In the upper right quadrant of the figure is the Cluster, its horseshoe-shaped, open mouth facing the paired, horseshoe-mouth of the Pleiades, found in the lower left quadrant. Each constellation has seven visible stars, so that they perfectly echo one another's open-mouthed circle. Moreover, the Cluster, being male, is properly larger than the smaller, female Pleiades.

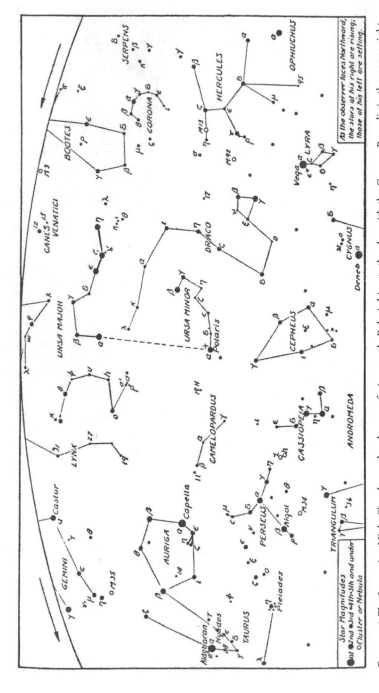

FIGURE 6: The Iroquoian Night Sky, shows the observer facing north. Polaris bisects the sky, with the Corona Borealis in the upper right quadrant and the Pleiades in the lower left quadrant. SOURCE: Kelvin McKready, *A Beginner's Star Book* (London: Putnam's, 1912) 4.

One of my favorite versions of the overhead view showing nested circles is found in Figure 7, Concentric Motif in Mound-Writing. Here, we are looking at the Lenape articulation of dimensional reality as onion-like, peeling inward from Sky to the central core of Earth.[18] Very interestingly, this is the basic design of the pre-contact, Aztec island city of Tenochtitlán, which sat in the middle of the Lake of the Moon, with its rings a series of alternating canals and land.[19] I cannot certainly say that Tenochtitlán's design was based on the same concept of Sky and Earth common to the eastern woodlands, but I do find its motif very suggestive. (It is well known that Central America also operated on complex binaries.)

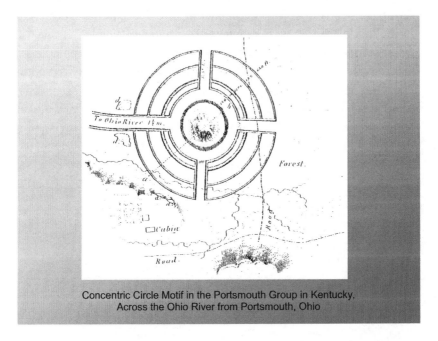

Concentric Circle Motif in the Portsmouth Group in Kentucky, Across the Ohio River from Portsmouth, Ohio

**FIGURE 7**: Concentric Motif in Mound-Writing, shows the top-down view of the Sky-Earth binary, as complicated in Lenape thought. SOURCE: Ephraim George Squier and E. H. Davis, *Ancient Monuments of the Mississippi Valley: Comprising the Results of Extensive Original Surveys and Explorations.* Smithsonian Contributions to Knowledge, 2 vols. (1848, reprint; New York: Johnson Reprint Corporation, 1965) 1:76, facing.

18. *Hitakonanu'laxk* [Tree Beard], *The Grandfathers Speak: Native American Folk Tales of the Lenape People* (New York: Interlink, 1994) 32.

19. David E. Stannard, *American Holocaust: The Conquest of the New World* (New York: Oxford University Press, 1992) 3–4.

## BINARY PATTERNS OF THINKING

What is demonstrated throughout woodlands culture, then, is an intense focus on reality as a set of binary complements, both spiritually and physically. Nothing could be singled out from a base-two unit for consideration in isolation. Such a concept is grasped only when both halves of each binary are fully represented, making one of anything a mere half, i.e., a *fraction* (½). In terms of spiritual discussions, this means that nothing is free-standing. There are no solitary units of "power," such as a monotheistic "god." Instead, there are many covalent spirits cooperating to create reality, each out of its appropriate Sky or Earth realm of existence.

The Christian-Native failure to communicate forms a self-sustaining feed-back loop. It arose from a complete mismatch of cultural expectations in the first place that was complicated by invasion-enabled evangelism in the second place, until academia sanctioned western interpolations as source material, in the third place. Throughout, true Native perceptions have been omitted from the monologue. Nothing will be lost by reinstating the old Native paradigms. Instead, the weight of linear western paradigms will be lifted from binary Native shoulders, enriching the discussion as the Other Half finally joins the conversation.

# PART TWO

# Re-Discovering the Concept of Discovery in the Christian Mission to Native America

3

# Christianity, American Indians, and the Doctrine of Discovery

ROBERT J. MILLER

*The European countries that explored and colonized North America utilized the international law Doctrine of Discovery to claim sovereign and human rights over the indigenous peoples. Discovery was developed primarily in the fifteenth century by England, Spain, Portugal, and the Church to control property acquisitions in non-European lands. The assumed superiority of European civilizations and religions was an element of the Doctrine. The U.S. Supreme Court adopted Discovery in 1823 in Johnson v. M'Intosh. Long before then, however, Discovery and Christian religions and civilizations influenced Euro-American interactions with the indigenous people. Starting with the fifteenth-century papal bulls and English Royal charters, including Jamestown's, the primary goals of colonization included "propagating Christian Religion" and bringing "human civility" to the "pagan," "heathen," "Infidels and Savages" who "yet live[d] in Darkness and miserable ignorance of the true Knowledge and Worship of God." These goals continued to be part of United States Indian policy and Manifest Destiny until nearly the end of the twentieth century.*

## INTRODUCTION

NORTH AMERICA WAS COLONIZED under an international legal principle called the Doctrine of Discovery. The Doctrine was created and justified by ethnocentric ideas of European and Christian superiority over the other cultures, religions, and peoples of the world.

Discovery provided that newly-arrived Europeans automatically acquired property rights in Native lands and gained governmental, religious, and commercial rights over the inhabitants.[1] When Europeans planted their flags and religious symbols in these newly discovered lands, they were not just thanking God for a safe voyage. Instead, they were undertaking well-recognized rituals of Discovery to make legal claims.[2] The United States also adopted Discovery and it is still being used against American Indians today.[3]

## THE DOCTRINE OF DISCOVERY AND CHRISTIANITY

Discovery was developed primarily in the fifteenth century by England, Spain, Portugal, and the Catholic Church to control acquisitions of non-European lands. The assumed superiority of European civilizations and religions was a major part of the Doctrine from the very beginning.

Long before the 1400s, however, various popes established the idea of a universal papal jurisdiction which "vested a legal responsibility in the pope to realize the vision of the universal Christian commonwealth."[4] The papal responsibility for God's earthly flock and the duty to increase that flock, led to the idea of holy war by Christians against infidels.[5]

But more specifically, the Doctrine has been traced to the Crusades to recover the Holy Lands in 1096–1271.[6] Scholars have cited Pope Innocent IV's commentary in 1240 in which he stated that it was legitimate for Christians to invade the lands of infidels because the Crusades

1. Johnson V. M'Intosh, 21 U.S. (8 Wheat.) (1823) 543.

2. Patricia Seed, *Ceremonies of Possession in Europe's Conquest of the New World, 1492-1640* (Cambridge: Cambridge University Press, 1995) 9 n. 19, 69–73, 101–2.

3. Robert J. Miller, *Native America, Discovered and Conquered: Thomas Jefferson, Lewis & Clark, and Manifest Destiny* (Lincoln: University Of Nebraska Press, 2008) 163–72.

4. Robert A. Williams Jr., *The American Indian in Western Legal Thought: The Discourses of Conquest* (New York: Oxford University Press, 1990) 29.

5. Williams, *American Indian in Western Legal Thought*, 29–31; Carl Erdmann, *The Origin of the Idea of Crusade*, trans. Marshall W. Baldwin and Walter Goffart (Princeton, NJ: Princeton University Press, 1977) 155–56.

6. Williams, *American Indian in Western Legal Thought*, 14. See also Anthony Pagden, *Lords of All the World: Ideologies of Empire in Spain, Britain And France c. 1500–c. 1800* (New Haven, CT: Yale University Press, 1995) 8, 24, 126; James Muldoon, ed., *The Expansion of Europe: The First Phase* (Philadelphia: University of Pennsylvania Press, 1977); and James A. Brundage, *Medieval Canon Law and the Crusader* (Madison: University of Wisconsin Press, 1969).

were just wars fought for the "defense" of Christianity.[7] Innocent focused on the legal question of the authority of Christians to dispossess pagans of their *dominium,* their sovereignty and property.[8] The Pope stated that non-Christian rights to sovereignty and property were qualified by the papacy's divine mandate.[9] Since the pope was entrusted with the spiritual health of all the human flock, that necessarily meant he had a voice in the secular affairs of all humans, and had the duty to intervene if infidels violated natural law, as that was defined by Europeans.[10]

The religious development of Discovery continued in the early 1400s in a controversy between Poland and the Teutonic Knights over non-Christian Lithuania.[11] In the Council of Constance of 1414, called to settle this dispute, the Knights claimed that papal bulls from the Crusades authorized their outright confiscation of heathen property and sovereignty.[12] The Council, however, accepted Poland's argument based on Innocent IV's argument that infidels possessed natural law rights but that the pope could order invasions to punish violations of natural law or to spread the Christian gospel.[13] Thus, future crusades, discoveries, and conquests of heathens would have to proceed under Innocent's legal rule that pagans had natural rights, but that they had to comply with European concepts of natural law and religion or risk subjugation.[14]

These principles were put into practice as Portugal and Spain began finding lands outside of Europe. In the mid-1400s, Spain and Portugal began to clash over the eastern Atlantic island groups. Portugal finally convinced Pope Eugenius IV that if Portugal colonized the

7. Miller, *Native America, Discovered and Conquered,* 12–13; Williams, *American Indian in Western Legal Thought,* 13.

8. Williams, *American Indian in Western Legal Thought,* 13 n. 4; Henry Wheaton, *Elements of International Law,* ed. William B. Lawrence, 6th ed. (Boston: Little Brown, 1855) 226–39.

9. Williams, *American Indian in Western Legal Thought,* 13.

10. Ibid., 14–17, 46–47, 66. Pagan nations that denied the Christian God and the universal authority of the Pope "were denied any legitimacy and their property and Lordship could rightfully be confiscated by crusading Christian armies" (Ibid., 49).

11. Ibid., 59–60.

12. Ibid., 62–63; James Muldoon, *Popes, Lawyers and Infidels: The Church and the Non-Christian World, 1250–1550* (Philadelphia: University of Pennsylvania Press, 1979) 109–19.

13. Williams, *American Indian in Western Legal Thought,* 65.

14. Ibid., 66–67; Muldoon, *Popes, Lawyers and Infidels,* 119.

Canary Islands it would be a conquest on behalf of Christianity.[15] The Portuguese conversion of the infidels was based on their non-Christian religion and their alleged lack of civilization.[16] The King even claimed that the Canary Island converts had now received the benefits of civilized laws and an organized society.[17] The King wanted to settle the Islands, he claimed, only to advance civilization and Christianity, "more indeed for the salvation of the souls of the pagans of the islands than for [the King's] personal gain."[18]

This dialogue led to a refinement in the Discovery principle. The new argument for European and Christian domination was not based on infidels' lack of *dominium* or natural rights but because of Portugal's obligations to lead them to Christianity. The Pope's lawyers agreed that under the Roman law of nations (*ius gentium*) infidels had a right to *dominium* although the papacy maintained an indirect jurisdiction over their secular activities. They cited Innocent IV that the Pope had authority to deprive pagans of their property and sovereignty if they failed to admit Christian missionaries or violated natural law.[19] The Pope then issued *Romanus Pontifex* in 1436 and authorized Portugal to convert the Canary Islanders and control the islands for the Pope.[20] This bull was reissued several times in the fifteenth century and extended Portugal's jurisdiction and geographical rights into Africa.[21] These decrees recognized the Pope's interest to bring all humankind "into the one fold of the Lord" and authorized Portugal's works of conversion and its title and sovereignty over the

15. Williams, *American Indian in Western Legal Thought*, 69.

16. Ibid., 69; Muldoon, *Expansion of Europe*, 54.

17. Williams, *American Indian in Western Legal Thought*, 69; Muldoon, *Expansion of Europe*, 55.

18. Muldoon, *Expansion of Europe*, 55–56.

19. Williams, *American Indian in Western Legal Thought*, 71–72; Muldoon, *Popes, Lawyers and Infidels*, 126–27.

20. Williams, *American Indian in Western Legal Thought*, 72.

21. Sidney Z. Ehler, ed., *Church and State through the Centuries: A Collection of Historic Documents with Commentaries*, trans. John B. Morrall (New York: Biblo & Tannen, 1967) 146–53. In 1455, Pope Nicholas authorized Portugal "to invade, search out, capture, vanquish, and subdue all Saracens and pagans" and place them into perpetual slavery and take all their property; see Frances G. Davenport, ed., *European Treaties Bearing on the History of the United States and Its Dependencies to 1648* (Washington, DC: Carnegie Institution of Washington, 1917) 23.

lands "which have already been acquired and which shall be acquired in the future."[22]

Catholic Spain utilized these same principles in sending Columbus westward. King Ferdinand and Queen Isabella sponsored Columbus' voyages under a contract that declared him the Admiral of any lands he would "discover and acquire."[23]

Columbus then took the Doctrine of Discovery to the New World and Spain wasted no time in seeking papal ratification of its claims. In 1493, Pope Alexander VI issued three bulls which confirmed Spain's title to these "new" discoveries.[24]

In *Inter caetera II*, Alexander drew a line, from pole to pole, 100 leagues west of the Azores, and granted Spain title under the authority of God to all the lands discovered or to be discovered west of the line. Portugal was granted the same rights east of the line. Spain was to carry out this "holy and laudable [conversion] work" to contribute to "the expansion of the Christian rule."[25]

Consequently, under the existing canon and European law, the Church's interest in expanding Christendom, and Spain's and Portugal's economic and political interests, the Doctrine of Discovery had solidified in 1493 to stand for four basic points. First, the Church had the authority to grant to Christian kings title and ownership of the lands of infidels. Second, European exploration facilitated the pope's guardianship duties over the earthly flock. Third, Spain and Portugal held exclusive rights over other European countries to colonize the world. Finally, mere discovery of new lands by Spain or Portugal in their respective spheres was sufficient to create these rights.[26]

A debate arose, however, as to the authority for Spain's rights in the New World. Ferdinand then asked for legal opinions on the legitimacy of

---

22. Ehler, *Church and State*, 146, 150.

23. Williams, *American Indian in Western Legal Thought*, 74–78; Samuel Eliot Morison, *Admiral of the Ocean Sea: A Life of Christopher Columbus* (Boston: Little Brown, 1942) 78, 105.

24. Davenport, *European Treaties*, 9–13, 23, 53–56—in *Inter Caetera Divinai* May 1493 the Pope ordered that the lands "undiscovered by others" belonged to Spain; Alexander also granted Spain any lands it might discover in the future provided they were "not previously possessed by any Christian owner."

25. Morison, *Admiral of the Ocean Sea*, 368–73; Ehler, *Church and State*, 156.

26. Pagden, *Lords of All the World*, 31–33; Muldoon, *Popes, Lawyers and Infidels*, 139.

relying on the papal bulls for Spain's title, and even convened a group to draft regulations to control future conquests.[27]

In 1532, a priest, University of Salamanca professor, and advisor to the king, Franciscus de Victoria, reached three conclusions regarding Spanish explorations. First, the Natives of the Americas "possessed natural legal rights as free and rational people." Second, the pope's grant of title to Spain could not affect the inherent rights of the Indians. Third, violations by the Indians of the natural-law principles of the Law of Nations (as determined of course by European Christian countries) justified a Christian nation's conquest and colonial empire in the New World.[28]

The first two conclusions seemed to reject Spain's title based solely on papal grants. However, what Victoria actually did was to strengthen the justification for Spain's empire from being based solely on papal grants to a firmer foundation based on the "universal obligations of a Eurocentrically constructed natural law."[29] In fact, Victoria reasoned that New World Natives were required to allow Spaniards to exercise their rights to travel, to engage in trade, to profit from items the Natives apparently held in common, and to send missionaries to preach the gospel.[30] Victoria's conclusion was that if infidels violated any of these natural law rights of the Spanish then Spain could "defend" its rights and fight a lawful and just war against the Natives.[31] Consequently, Victoria limited the

27. Pagden, *Lords of All the World*, 46; Williams, *American Indian in Western Legal Thought*, 89–91. The new regulation was the *Requerimiento*. It informed new world Natives that they must accept Spanish missionaries and sovereignty or be annihilated. It was required to be read to Natives before warfare could legally ensue. It informed them of their obligation to hear the gospel, and that their territory had been donated to Spain. If the Natives refused to acknowledge the church, the king, and to admit priests, then Spain was justified in making war on them. See Muldoon, *Popes, Lawyers and Infidels*, 141–42; Seed, *Ceremonies of Possession*, 69–73; Lewis Hanke, *The Spanish Struggle for Justice in the Conquest of America* (Philadelphia: University of Pennsylvania Press, 1949) 33; and Charles Gibson, ed., *The Spanish Tradition in America* (New York: Harper & Row, 1968) 59–60.

28. Franciscus De Victoria, *De Indis Et De Iure Bellie: Relectiones*, ed., Ernest Nys, trans. John Pauley Bate (Washington, DC: Carnegie Institution of Washington, 1917) 115, 123, 125–28, 151, 153; Williams, *American Indian in Western Legal Thought*, 97–101.

29. Williams, *American Indian in Western Legal Thought*, 98.

30. De Victoria, *De Indis*, 151–61; Williams, *American Indian in Western Legal Thought*, 101–03; Arthur Nussbaum, *A Concise History of the Law of Nations* (New York: Macmillan, 1947) 61–62: Victoria "considers interference with the preaching of the gospel as a just cause of war."

31. De Victoria, *De Indis*, 54–55; Seed, *Ceremonies of Possession*, 88–97; Pagden, *Lords*

natural law freedoms of American Indians by allowing Spain's natural law rights to trump Native interests.

England and France also participated in the development of Discovery. Both countries utilized the international Doctrine of Discovery and claimed the rights and powers of first discovery in North America. England, for example, claimed that John Cabot's 1496–1498 alleged first discoveries from Newfoundland to Virginia gave it priority over any other European country.[32] In turn, France vigorously contested England's claims of first discovery in North America. The French pointed to their alleged first discoveries as establishing their Discovery claim to ownership and sovereignty.[33]

France and England, however, faced a common problem regarding colonization because they both were Catholic countries in 1493. Their kings were very concerned with infringing Spain's rights, violating the papal bulls, and risking excommunication.[34] Yet, they were also hungry to get their share of the spoils. Hence, the legal scholars of England and France devised new theories of Discovery that allowed their countries to colonize the New World.

They determined that the Catholic King Henry VII would not violate the 1493 papal bulls if English explorers restrained themselves to lands not yet discovered by any other Christian prince. This expanded definition of Discovery was further refined by Elizabeth I to require current occupancy and actual possession of land by Europeans as crucial elements of Discovery. Consequently, Henry VII, Elizabeth I, and James I repeatedly

---

*of All the World*, 93, 97–98 (defending the faith was one Spanish rationale for a just war); Hanke, *Spanish Struggle for Justice*, 133–46, 156–72.

32. Pagden, *Lords of All the World*, 90; Williams, *American Indian in Western Legal Thought*, 161, 170, 177–78; and Alden T. Vaughan and Barbara Graymont, eds., *Early American Indian Documents: Treaties And Laws, 1607–1789*, vol. 7: *New York and New Jersey treaties, 1609–1682* (1985; reprint, Bethesda, MD: University Publications of America, 1998) 30–32.

33. Pagden, *Lords of All the World*, 34; Joseph Jouvency, *Canadicae missionis relatio ab anno 1611 usque ad annum 1613 cum statu ejusdem missionis, annis 1703 & 1710* (Romae: Ex typographia Georgii Plachi, 1710) 179, 205; and Reuben Gold Thwaites, ed., *The Jesuit Relations and Allied Documents: Travels and Explorations of the Jesuit Missionaries in New France, 1610–1791* (New York: Pageant, 1959) 33, 127, 199, 203.

34. Williams, *American Indian in Western Legal Thought*, 74, 81.

instructed their explorers to discover and colonize lands "unknown to all Christians" and lands "not actually possessed of any Christian prince."[35]

England and France also developed a cultural justification for Discovery claims over Native peoples. They developed the principle of *terra nullius* that lands that were not possessed by anyone, or which were occupied by non-Europeans but not being used in a fashion that European legal systems approved, were waste or vacant.[36] France, England, and the American colonies and the United States often used this argument because they claimed American Indians used land only for hunting and left it as wilderness.

The Crown also relied on religion to justify its claims in the New World. Henry VII ordered the Cabots "to seek out and discover all . . . provinces whatsoever, that may belong to heathens and infidels" and "to subdue, occupy, and possess these territories. . . ." Elizabeth I granted Sir Humphrey Gilbert the right to "discover such remote heathen and barbarous lands, counties, and territories, not actually possessed by any Christian prince or people, and to hold occupy and enjoy the same, with all . . . jurisdictions. . . ." James I went further and granted his colonists property rights in America because the lands were "not now actually possessed by any *Christian* Prince or People" and "there is noe other the Subjects of any Christian King or State . . . actually in Possession . . . whereby any Right, Claim, Interest, or Title, may . . . by that Meanes accrue." James I also ordered his colonists to convert American Indians to Christianity: "propagate[e] *Christian* Religion to those [who] as yet live in Darkness and miserable Ignorance of the true Knowledge and Worship of God, and

35. Francis Jennings, *The Invasion of America: Indians, Colonialism and the Cant of the Conquest* (Chapel Hill, NC: Institute of Early American History and Culture, University of North Carolina Press, 1975) 132; cf. Henry VII to John Cabot 1496, and 1620 Patent of New England by King James I, both in W. Keith Kavenagh, ed., *Foundations of Colonial America: A Documentary History*, 3 vols. (New York: Chelsea, 1973) 1:18, 22–29; and Elizabeth I to Humphrey Gilbert 1578, to Walter Raleigh 1583, and Charter of Virginia 1606, all in Kavenagh, ed., *Foundations of Colonial America*, 2:1690–98.

36. *Terra Nullius* essentially ignored the title of original inhabitants based on subjective assessments of their level of civilization; cf. Alex C. Castles, *An Australian Legal History* (Sydney: Law, 1982) 63, reprinted in Heather McRae, Garth Nettheim, and Laura Beacroft, eds., *Aboriginal Legal Issues: Commentary and Materials* (North Ryde, NSW, Australia: Law, and Holmes Beach, FL: Gaunt, 1991) 10. The term has two meanings: "a country without a sovereign recognized by European authorities and a territory where nobody owns any land at all"; see Henry Reynolds, *The Law of the Land* (New York: Viking Penguin, 1987) 173.

[to] bring the Infidels and Savages, living in those Parts, to human civility, and to a settled and quiet Government. . . ."[37]

## THE MODERN DEFINITION OF DISCOVERY

In 1823, in *Johnson v. M'Intosh*,[38] the U.S. Supreme Court held that Discovery was an established legal principle of English colonial law and American law.[39] In a nutshell, Discovery meant that when European Christian nations encountered new lands that the discovering country automatically gained property rights over non-Christian nations even though the Native people already owned, occupied, and were using their lands.[40] In addition, the discovering country also gained governmental rights over the Native people and their governments which restricted tribal international political relationships and trade.

The Supreme Court stated that "discovery gave title to the government by whose subjects, or by whose authority, it was made against all other European governments, which title might be consummated by possession."[41] Native property rights, however, were "in no instance, entirely disregarded; but were necessarily, to a considerable extent, impaired."[42] This was so because the Doctrine recognized that Natives still held a right to occupy and use their lands but "their rights to complete sovereignty, as independent nations, were necessarily diminished, and their power to dispose of the soil at their own will, to whomsoever they pleased, was denied by the original fundamental principle, that discovery gave exclusive title to those who made it."[43]

I have identified ten distinct elements of the Doctrine.[44]

---

37. See Kavenagh, ed., *Foundations*, 1:18, 22–29, and 2:1690–98; cf. William Macdonald, ed., *Select Charters and Other Documents Illustrative of American History 1606–1775* (1906; reprint, Littleton, CO: Rothman, 1993) 2–3, 18, 24–25, 37–39, 51–52, 59, 121–26, 184, 205.

38. Johnson, 21 U.S., 543.

39. Johnson, 21 U.S., 571. The case concerned land purchases made in 1773 and 1775 by British citizens.

40. Johnson, 21 U.S., 573–74.

41. Johnson, 21 U.S., 573; accord id. at 574, 584, 588, 592, 603.

42. Johnson, 21 U.S., 574.

43. Johnson, 21 U.S., 574.

44. Miller, *Native America, Discovered and Conquered*, 3–5.

1. *Christianity.* Religion was a significant aspect of the Doctrine. Under Discovery, non-Christian peoples did not have the same rights to land, sovereignty, and self-determination as Christians.

2. *Civilization.* The Euro-American definition of civilization was an important part of Discovery and of ideas of Euro-American superiority. Euro-Americans thought that God had directed them to bring civilized ways, education, and religion to indigenous peoples and to exercise paternalistic and guardianship powers over them.

3. *First discovery.* The first European country to discover lands unknown to other Europeans gained property and sovereign rights over the lands and peoples.

4. *Actual occupancy and current possession.* To acquire complete title, a discovering country had to actually occupy and possess the newly found lands, usually by building forts or settlements.

5. *Preemption.* The discovering country gained the power of preemption, that is, the sole right to buy the lands from the Native people.

6. *Indian title.* Indian Nations were considered by Euro-American legal systems to have lost the full ownership of their lands. They only retained occupancy and use rights.

7. *Tribal limited sovereign and commercial rights.* Indian Nations and Native peoples were considered to have lost some of their sovereignty and rights to international trade and diplomacy. Thereafter, they could only deal with the Euro-American government that had discovered them.

8. *Contiguity.* Europeans claimed a significant amount of land surrounding their settlements. The discovery of the mouth of a river, for example, created a claim over the entire drainage system. Notice the shapes of the Louisiana Territory and Oregon Country.

9. *Terra nullius.* The phrase means a land that is void or empty. If lands were not occupied by any people or were being used in a fashion that Euro-American legal systems disapproved, then the lands were available for Discovery claims.

10. *Conquest.* This element has two meanings as described in *Johnson*. The Court defined military victory in "just" and necessary wars as one way to acquire the Indian title. But conquest also described the

property rights that Europeans gained automatically by first discovery; in essence, the first discovery was like a military conquest.

The Supreme Court expressly used the two elements that we are focusing on, Christianity and civilization, to justify Discovery. According to the Court, the Doctrine of Discovery applied in the New World because of the different cultures, religions, and savageness of Native Americans.

> On the discovery of this immense continent, the great nations of Europe were eager to appropriate to themselves so much of it as they could respectively acquire. Its vast extent offered an ample field to the ambition and enterprise of all; and *the character and religion* of its inhabitants afforded an apology for considering them as a people over whom *the superior genius of Europe* might claim an ascendency. The potentates of the old world found no difficulty in convincing themselves that they made *ample compensation* to the inhabitants of the new, by bestowing on them *civilization and Christianity*, in exchange for unlimited independence.[45]

The Court also added: "Although we do not mean to engage in the defence of those principles which Europeans have applied to Indian title, they may, we think, find *some excuse, if not justification, in the character and habits of the people whose rights have been wrested from them.*"[46]

## DISCOVERY IN THE AMERICAN STATES

It is no surprise that European civilizations and religions were used by the English colonies and later American governments. The Puritans, for example, felt that "they were charged with a special spiritual and political destiny, to create in the New World a church and a society that would provide the model for all the nations of Europe. . . ."[47]

The English colonial governments assumed that the Crown held the Discovery power and that the colonies were authorized to conduct political affairs and commercial transactions with Indian Nations under this

45. Johnson, 21 U.S., 573, italics added. Ironically, Indians were considered compensated for their loss of property and sovereignty with the very two things responsible for justifying that loss, civilization and religion.

46. Johnson, 21 U.S., 589, italics added. One author alleges that the Old Testament is the background for Johnson v. M'intosh; cf. Steven T. Newcomb, *Pagans in the Promised Land: Decoding the Doctrine of Christian Discovery* (Golden, CO: Fulcrum, 2008) xv.

47. Deborah L. Madsen, *American Exceptionalism* (Edinburgh: Edinburgh University Press, 1998) 1.

royal authority. All thirteen colonies enacted numerous laws exercising Discovery powers to purchase Indian lands and to protect the colonial right of preemption and sovereignty over tribes. The colonies repeatedly relied on religion, cultural differences, and "civilization" to justify their claims over Indians.[48]

The new American state governments that formed after the Revolution immediately utilized Discovery. The states began adopting constitutions and enacting statutes in which they asserted the same powers and superiority over Indians that they had claimed during colonial times. In fact, several states immediately enshrined the Doctrine of Discovery in their new constitutions and laws.[49]

In 1835, for example, the Tennessee Supreme Court upheld the authority of the state to extend criminal jurisdiction into Indian country. The court relied on the elements of Discovery and "the law of Christendom" to hold that the state possessed sovereign power over Indians, "the unconverted natives."[50] A concurring justice also raised the idea of "just war" and wrote that if Indian tribes resisted Americans taking their lands that Americans could "use force to repel such resistance."[51]

In 1813, the Pennsylvania Supreme Court stated that Indians could not own real property since "not being Christians, but mere heathens [they are] unworthy of the earth."[52] And, in 1808, the New York Supreme Court used cultural justifications to denigrate the Mohawk Nation's ownership of land because the tribe's "wandering and unsettled life" was "wholly in-

---

48. Miller, *Native America, Discovered and Conquered*, 25–33; Francis Paul Prucha, *The Great Father: The United States Government and the American Indians* (1984; reprint, Lincoln, NE: University of Nebraska Press, 1995) 116, 120.

49. See, e.g., N.Y. Const. Art. 37 (1777); N.C. Const. Art. I, § 25 (1776); Ga. Const. Art. I, § 23 (1798); John D. Cushing, ed., *The First Laws of the State of Virginia* (1785; reprint, Wilmington, DE: Glazier, 1982) 35, 104; John D. Cushing, ed., *The First Laws of the State of Connecticut* (1784; reprint, Wilmington, DE: Glazier, 1982) 101–2; John D. Cushing, ed., *The First Laws of the State of North Carolina* (1784; reprint, Wilmington, DE: Glazier, 1984) 446.

50. Tennessee v. Forman, 16 Tenn. (1835), 256, 258–85, 287, 332–35; "The principle declared in the fifteenth century as the law of Christendom, that discovery gave title to assume sovereignty over, and to govern the unconverted natives of Africa, Asia, and North and South America, has been recognized as a part of the national law, for nearly four centuries" (277).

51. 16 Tenn., 339–40.

52. Thompson v. Johnston, 6 Binn. 68, 1813 WL 1243 (Pa. Sup. Ct. 1813) 2, 5.

consistent with the idea of a permanent . . . possession."[53] These judicial statements demonstrate graphically the religious and cultural bias that lurks behind the Doctrine of Discovery.

The evidence proves that the United States also adopted the Doctrine of Discovery and its justifications of culture, civilization, and Christianity to exercise sovereign, cultural, and religious dominance over Indian Nations.[54] In the Northwest Ordinance of 1787, for example, designed to open the Ohio area to settlement, the Articles of Confederation Congress expressly adopted Discovery: "The utmost good faith shall always be observed towards the Indians, their lands and property shall never be taken from them without their consent; and in their property, rights and liberty, they shall never be invaded or disturbed, unless in just and lawful wars. . . ."[55] This statute expressly required consent for sales of tribal lands, exercised the government's exclusive preemption power, and raised the specter of "just war."

In 1790, our first Congress under the U.S. Constitution expressly adopted Discovery and preemption:

> [N]o sale of lands made by an Indian, or any nation or tribe of Indians within the United States, shall be valid to any person or persons, or to any state, whether having the right of pre-emption to such lands or not, unless the same shall be made and duly executed at some public treaty, held under the authority of the United States.[56]

And, the U.S. Supreme Court expressly adopted Discovery as American law in *Johnson v. M'Intosh* in 1823 and relied on its elements of civilization and Christianity to claim superior property and sovereign rights over Native people.

## MANIFEST DESTINY

Historians state that Manifest Destiny is exemplified by three basic aspects: First, the United States has unique moral virtues that other coun-

---

53. Jackson, Ex Dem. J. G. Klock and G. G. Klock v. Hudson, 3 Johns. 375, 1808 WL 477, 3 Am. Dec. 500 (N.Y. Sup. Ct. 1808) 5.

54. Miller, *Native America, Discovered and Conquered*, 38–48, 59–76.

55. Francis Paul Prucha, *Documents of United States Indian Policy*, 3rd ed. (Lincoln: University of Nebraska Press, 2000) 9.

56. Act of July 22, 1790, Ch. 23, 1 Stat. 137, 138, §4.

tries do not possess. Second, the United States has a mission to redeem the world by spreading democracy and the American way of life around the globe. Third, America has a divinely ordained destiny to accomplish these tasks.[57] This kind of thinking arises from an ethnocentric view that one's own culture, government, race, religion, and country are superior to all others. This kind of thinking justified and motivated the development of Discovery in the fifteenth century and the idea of Manifest Destiny in the nineteenth century.

The phrase Manifest Destiny was first used in 1845 in editorials about the U.S. expanding into Texas and Oregon. In December 1845, an editorial about the Oregon country entitled "The True Title," expressly used civilization and Christianity to argue that the United States owned Oregon.

> Our *legal title* to Oregon, so far as law exists for such rights, is perfect. . . . we have a still better title than any that can ever be constructed out of all these antiquated materials of *old black-letter international law.* Away, away with all these cobweb tissues of *right of discovery, exploration, settlement, continuity,* & . . . our claim to Oregon . . . is by the right of our *manifest destiny to overspread and to possess the whole of the continent* which *Providence has given us* for the development of the great experiment of liberty and fed-erated self-government entrusted to us. . . . [In England's hands, Oregon] must always remain wholly useless and worthless for any purpose of human *civilization* or society. . . . The *God of nature and of nations* has marked it for our own; and with His blessing we will firmly maintain the incontestable rights He has given, and fearlessly perform the high duties He has imposed.[58]

Religion continued to play a major role in American expansion as missionaries helped lead the way across the continent. The federal gov-ernment used different Christian religions to control Indians, to educate them in boarding schools, to teach them civilization and religion, and to manage the reservations. The Bureau of Indian Affairs outlawed many

57. William Earl Weeks, *Building the Continental Empire: American Expansion from the Revolution to the Civil War* (Chicago: Ivan R. Dee, 1996) 60–61, 110; Charles L. Sanford, *Manifest Destiny and the Imperialism Question* (New York: Wiley, 1974) 10; Reginald Horsman, *Race and Manifest Destiny: The Origins of American Racial Anglo-Saxonism* (Cambridge: Harvard University Press, 1981) 86.

58. *New York Morning News,* 27 December 1845, quoted in Julius W. Pratt, "The Origin of 'Manifest Destiny,'" *American Historical Review* 32 (July 1927) 795, 796; italics added.

Indian religious ceremonies and tried to stamp out Indian culture and religion.[59] Indian children were even forced to practice Christian religions in the boarding schools.[60]

In 1882, a U.S. Indian commissioner reported: "One very important auxiliary in transforming men from savage to civilized life is the influence brought to bear upon them through the labors of Christian men and women as educators and missionaries. . . . Civilization is a plant of exceeding slow growth, unless supplemented by Christian teaching and influences. . . . [Only in this way] can our Indian population be so speedily and permanently reclaimed from the barbarism, idolatry, and savage life."[61]

## CONCLUSION

Their low estimation of the civilizations and religions of native people led them to allege Anglo-American superiority over indigenous cultures. They relied heavily on the civilizations and religions of Native people to claim an alleged superiority of Anglo-Americans. Apparently, Euro-Americans possessed the only valid religions, civilizations, governments, and cultures, and Providence intended that they own and dominate North America.

The Doctrine of Discovery is not just an esoteric relic of our history. It continues to impact Indian people and governments in the U.S. and indigenous peoples around the world today.[62] The Doctrine continues to play a very significant role in American Indian law and policies because it still restricts Indian people and Indian Nations in their property, gov-

59. *Felix Cohen's Handbook of Federal Indian Law* (1942; reprint, Albuquerque: University of New Mexico Press, 1971) 175 n. 345 and 176 n. 347; Robert J. Miller, "Exercising Cultural Self-Determination: The Makah Indian Tribe Goes Whaling," *American Indian Law Review* 25 (2001) 165, 199–204; and Carroll Riley, "The Makah Indians: A Study of Political And Economic Organization," *Ethnohistory* 15 (1968) 65 n. 5—the U.S. attacked "the religious and social parts of the culture."

60. Jay B. Nash, Oliver La Farge, and W. Carson Ryan, eds., *The New Day for the Indians: A Survey of the Working of the Indian Reorganization Act of 1934* (New York: Academy, 1938) 12.

61. Prucha, *Documents of United States Indian Policy*, 157.

62. Robert J. Miller and Jacinta Ruru, *An Indigenous Lens into Comparative Law: The Doctrine of Discovery in the United States and New Zealand* (2008), available at http://Papers.Ssrn.Com/Sol3/Papers.Cfm?Abstract_Id=1099574.

ernmental, and self-determination rights.[63] The cultural, racial, and religious justifications that led to the development of Discovery raise serious doubts about continuing to apply the Doctrine in modern-day American Indian law.

Four statements aptly sum up what Discovery meant for American Indians. In 1825, Secretary of State Henry Clay stated that it was "impossible to civilize Indians. . . . They were destined to extinction. . . ." When Senator Thomas Hart Benton was asked in the 1830s whether American expansion would cause the extinction of Indians if they "resisted civilization . . . [he said] I cannot murmur at what seems to be the effect of divine law. . . . The moral and intellectual superiority of the White race will do the rest. . . ." As Americans clashed with Indians in Wyoming in 1870, a newspaper noted: "The rich and beautiful valleys of Wyoming are destined for the occupancy and sustenance of the Anglo-Saxon race. . . . The Indians must stand aside or be overwhelmed. . . . The destiny of the aborigines is written in characters not to be mistaken . . . the doom of extinction is upon the red men of America." And, finally, an international law scholar stated in the mid-1800s what the Doctrine of Discovery did to indigenous people: "the heathen nations of the other quarters of the globe were the lawful spoil and prey of their civilized conquerors."[64]

## POSTSCRIPT

The Episcopal Church adopted a resolution entitled "Repudiate the Doctrine of Discovery" during its 76th General Convention in July 2009. The resolution states that Discovery creates "destructive policies . . . that lead to the colonizing dispossession of the lands of indigenous peoples and the disruption of their way of life. . . ." The Church calls on the United States to review its "historical and contemporary policies that contribute to the continuing colonization of Indigenous Peoples" and for Queen

63. Miller, *Native America, Discovered and Conquered*, 163–72.

64. Sanford, *Manifest Destiny and the Imperialism Question*, 46, 70; Horsman, *Race and Manifest Destiny*, 1, 3, 5, 110, 195, 300–303; Anders Stephanson, *Manifest Destiny: American Expansion and the Empire of Right* (New York: Hill & Wang, 1995) 54–57; Thomas R. Hietla, "'This Splendid Juggernaut': Westward a Nation and Its People," in *Manifest Destiny and Empire: American Antebellum Expansionism*, ed. Sam W. Haynes and Christopher Morris (College Station: The University of Texas at Arlington/Texas A&M University Press, 1997) 53; Henry Wheaton, *Elements of International Law*, 3rd ed. (Philadelphia: Lea & Blanchard, 1846) 210.

Elizabeth II to "disavow, and repudiate publicly, the claimed validity of the Christian Doctrine of Discovery. . . ." Will Christian churches and governments around the world take up this call to review their use of the Doctrine of Discovery against Indigenous peoples?[65]

Step → 127

65. Robert J. Miller, "Will Others Follow Episcopal Church's lead?" in *Indian Country Today* (August 12, 2009) 5; see also Judy Harrison, "Maine Episcopalians Move to Back Tribes," in *Bangor Daily News* (July 23, 2009), also available at http://bdn.new.adqic .com/detail/111303.html (last accessed August 6, 2009). For a copy of the resolution, see http://www.episcopalarchives.org/GC2009/09_nic/2009-D035.pdf (last accessed August 6, 2009).

4

# Colonial Virginia Mission Attitudes toward Native Peoples and African-American Slaves

EDWARD L. BOND

*One of the goals of the Jamestown venture was to convert Native Americans to Protestant Christianity. Although many people look back on this today with some degree of cynicism, the goal was sincerely held by many individuals who supported colonization and by some leading colonists. Nonetheless, the process by which the Virginia settlers were to attract converts—a process perhaps best described as "cultural conversion," in which Natives became English before they became Christian—proved unsuccessful. Combined with the Powhatan uprising of 1622, the mission to Virginia's Natives collapsed for all intents and purposes. Efforts to convert Africans and African Americans to Christianity also showed few indications of success. Even after a law passed in the 1660s declared that baptism did not change an individual's status as a slave, slave-owners were reluctant to allow ministers to baptize or proselytize their bondsmen and women. In the nineteenth century, when Episcopal ministers did succeed in converting some slaves, those individuals soon preferred the Baptist or Methodists churches to the Episcopal Church.*

## INTRODUCTION

THIS ESSAY FOCUSES ON the Church of England's mission to people in colonial Virginia. For the purposes of this book, however, mission means primarily the Christian mission to African Americans and Native Americans, thus excluding the large and relatively successful mission of the English Church to English Christians in North America. Yet even this smaller topic is an immense one, and one chapter cannot cover it adequately. Nor does it allow space to address the mission to slaves in the Antebellum period; the emergence of the African Methodist Episcopal Church; St. Phillips, New York City, and other African American Episcopal churches; or the efforts of evangelical Christians to spread the Gospel among slaves and Native Americans. Still, in keeping with the focus of this volume, the pages that follow discuss English efforts to spread the Gospel among Native Americans and African and later African American slaves, highlighting the changes in mission strategy over time.

## CHRISTIAN MISSION TO NATIVE AMERICANS

No single motive adequately explains English efforts to establish a colony in Virginia. Wealth, fame, and spreading the Gospel all played a role in the venture. Writing in 1609, two years after the settlement of Jamestown, the Reverend Robert Gray outlined several of the reasons: "Our land hath not milke sufficient in the breast thereof to nourish all those children which it hath brought forth. . . . And seeing there is neither preferment nor employment for all within the lists of our countrey, we might justly be accounted as in former times, both impudent and improuident, if we will yet sit with our armes foulded in or bosomes, and not rather seek after such aduentures whereby the glory of God may be aduanced, the territo-ries of our kingdome inlarged, our people both preferred and employed abroad."[1] There was nothing novel to his characterization. It included a familiar litany of motives common to the literature of the Jamestown venture: England was overpopulated and needed a place for its excess popu-lation, the New World provided a source of wealth, a colony would project English power, and converting the Natives would expand the kingdom of God. Gray's words offered not only an indictment of the English people for laziness but also a call for heroic action on behalf of both church and state. With Protestant heroes no longer dying at the stake, Gray chal-lenged a new generation of heroic Protestants to brave the dangers of an Atlantic voyage in order to establish a Christian polity in North America, to redeem the continent, and to convert the naturals of the land to true religion by acting upon the Great Commission in Matthew's Gospel. "It

---

1. Robert Gray, *A Good Speed to Virginia*, ed. Wesley Craven (1609; reprint, New York: Scholars' Facsimiles & Reprints, 1937) B-3.

is everie mans dutie," he wrote, "to trauell both by sea and land and to venture either with his person or with his purse, to bring the barbarous and sauage people to a ciuill and Christian kind of gouernment, under which they may learne how to live holily, iustly, and soberly in this world, and to apprehend the meanes to saue their soules in the world to come, rather than to destroy them."[2] William Crashaw made the same point in 1610, linking the Great Commission to the efforts of those who had first converted the English to Christianity: "the duty of all men who taste of that love; when they are converted they must labour the conversion of others."[3] The author of *A True and Sincere Declaration of the Purpose and Ends of the Plantation begun in Virginia* also indicated the reasons for planting colonies: "first to preach, & baptize into Christian Religion, and by propagation of that Gospell, to recouer out of the armies of the Diuell, a number of poore and miserable soules, wrapt vpp vnto death, in almost inuincible ignorance."[4]

England's mission to the New World was also part crusade. North America's bountiful forests, teeming rivers, and abundant plant and animal life made it easy for the Virginia Company of London to describe the continent as Eden or as the promised land of Canaan, a particularly apt image for people like the English who thought of themselves as God's early modern chosen people. Before it was Canaan, however, North America was one of the dark places of the earth. A vast English literature on demonology taught that Satan reigned in the world's remote and primitive territories. James I lent additional authority to this opinion nearly a decade before he ascended to the English throne when he wrote that such "wild partes of the world" were imbued with the presence of evil. And colonists did not dispute the assumption that early seventeenth-century Virginia was one of the "wild partes of the world."[5] A prayer

2. Ibid., C-2.

3. William Crashaw, *A Sermon Preached in London before the Right Honorable the Lord La Warre* (London, 1610) A-2. See also in the same discourse, C-3: "the principal ends [of the Virginia colony] being the plantation of a Church of English christians there, and consequently the conversion of the heathen from the divel to God."

4. Quoted in Peter Harrison, "'Fill the Earth and Subdue It': Biblical Warrants for Colonization in Seventeenth-Century England," no pagination, Faculties of Humanities and Social Sciences: Humanities and Social Sciences Papers, ePublications@bond, http://epublications.bond.edu.au/hss pubs/54 (accessed 9 September 2009). This is a significant paper that addresses topics raised by several essays in this collection.

5. Richard Beale Davis, "The Devil in Virginia in the Seventeenth Century," in

repeated daily at the beginning of each new watch borrowed from the Book of Revelation to describe North America as a dangerous part of the world ruled by an equally dangerous supernatural being: "the place where satans throne is."[6] William Crashaw, a Church of England minister and member of the Virginia Company of London, held similar sentiments. He wrote darkly of the continent in 1610, referring to it as the devil's "ancient freehold."[7] Speaking of Virginia in language that described Satan's aristocratic land rights or his kingship implied that colonization was part of a rescue mission to territory cursed by an evil landlord. Settlers acted as crusaders by leading a spiritual assault on the devil's dominion. By successfully establishing a colony in Virginia, English settlers redeemed the land. Another minister, the Reverend Patrick Copeland, described this action in 1622 when he alluded to Virginia as "that Heathen-now Christian Kingdome."[8]

English settlers participated in a second, more prominent, mission in North America—to the Natives of the land. They referred to this work in a variety of ways: as a Christian duty required of all adherents of the faith, as a means of repaying the Romans who first brought Christianity and civilization to the ancient Britons, and as a good work that would add to the rewards of the proselytizers in heaven.[9] The undertaking, however, was extraordinarily dangerous.

If Satan indeed ruled North America, then common sense implied that his reign extended over the people of the land as well. Either out of choice or fear the indigenous peoples must have been his subjects. The colonists knew that men did not have to worship the God of Christianity.

---

Virginia Magazine of History and Biography 65 (1957) 131; see Perry Miller, "Religion and Society in the Early Literature of Virginia," in Errand into the Wilderness, ed. Perry Miller (Cambridge: Belknap Press of Harvard University Press, 1956) 114, and William Strachey, Historie of Travell in Virginia Britania, ed. Louis B. Wright (1612; reprint, London: Hakluyt Society, 1952) 99–100.

6. For the Colony in Virginiea Britannia: Lawes Divine, Morall and Martiall, &c. (London, 1612), reprinted in Peter Force, ed., Tracts and Other Papers, Relating Principally to the Origin, Settlement, and Progress of the Colonies in North America, 4 vols. (Washington, DC: by the editor, 1844) 3 n. 2, 67.

7. Crashaw, Sermon Preached in London, H-1.

8. Patrick Copeland, Virginia's God be Thanked (London, 1622) 2.

9. For a good overview of Anglican efforts to convert Native Americans, see Owanah Anderson, 400 Years: Anglican/Episcopal Mission among Native Americans (Cincinnati: Forward Movement Publications, 1997).

Ignorance or willful perversion could lead men and women to pay homage to the devil instead, an abomination that Christian groups routinely accused their opponents of practicing. Protestants claimed it of Roman Catholics; Roman Catholics claimed it of Protestants; and Christians of all persuasions believed devil worship played a central role in Native American culture. Francis Magnel, an Irishman who accompanied the first voyage to Jamestown wrote of North America: "There they worship the Devil, whom they hold for their God, and they say that he talks to them often, appearing in human shape."[10]

Native American appearances confirmed English suspicions that the Indians enjoyed a close relationship with Satan by making possible an invidious connection between body and spirit. Colonial leaders who had read deeply in the era's manuals of gentility, which emphasized the physical presentation of the human form, would have seen in Native bodies something approaching their ideal. They admired the Natives' well proportioned and finely toned physiques as extraordinary examples of God's handiwork. John Smith's description of a Susquehannock was typical: "the goodliest man that ever we beheld."[11] Yet, the Natives intentionally marred their bodies in grotesque ways and covered themselves with hideous costumes that perverted the image of their maker, "fashion[ing] themselves as neare as possible" to the shape of their own deity, the devil, in attempts to emulate his appearance, thus making their bodies macabre visual statements of the medieval doctrine that like would know like.[12] They decorated their bodies with elaborate tattoos of serpents and wild beasts. To colonists used to English standards, Native Americans present-

10. Francis Magnel, "Francis Magnels' Relation of the First Voyage and Beginning of the Jamestown Colony," in *The Jamestown Voyages under the First Charter, 1606–1609*, 2 vols., ed. Phillip L. Barbour (Cambridge: Cambridge University Press, 1969) 1:154. See also Keith Thomas, *Religion and the Decline of Magic: Studies in Popular Beliefs in Sixteenth and Seventeenth Century England* (London: Weidenfeld & Nicolson, 1971) 477.

11. Karen Ordahl Kupperman, *Settling with the Indians: The Meeting of English and Indian Cultures in North America, 1580–1640* (Totawa, NJ: Rowman & Littlefield, 1980) 37; see also Kupperman, "Presentments of Civility: English Readings of Self-Presentation in the Early Years of Colonization," in *William and Mary Quarterly* 3rd ser. 54 (1997) 198.

12. Edward L. Bond, "Source of Knowledge, Source of Power: The Supernatural World of English Virginia, 1607–1624," in *Virginia Magazine of History and Biography* 108 (2000) 117–18.

ed an inverted image of beauty: "he is the most gallant who is the most monstrous to behold."[13]

Colonial accounts of Native bodies carried implications beyond mere physical descriptions, however, for English philosophy and theology linked body and spirit by suggesting that the exterior appearance of the body provided evidence of the interior state of the soul. Thus, when John Smith referred to Powhatan as "more like a devil then a man[,] with some two hundred more as blacke as himselfe,"[14] or when George Percy described the Natives as "so many Wolves or Devils,"[15] they were not just comparing the Natives to frightening beasts or to terrifying supernatural forces. They were also saying that Native Americans' hideous appearances were outward manifestations of disfigured souls. Native self-presentments became ontological statements suggesting their subjection to Satan.

English Protestant observers also tended to understand Native religion through the lens of Roman Catholicism. They referred to Native religious leaders, for instance, as "priests." This was by no means a neutral term used to describe a religious leader; when used by Protestants the word hinted of something more ominous. For Protestants the "priest" was a term of reproach that implied idleness, manipulation, and corruption. Alexander Whitaker attributed to Native priests diabolical parentage, subtlety, and deadly attacking abilities before comparing them to monks living cloistered in monasteries and to snakes that only left their hiding places in order to strike quickly and poison their victims: "[their priests] are a generation of vipers even of Sathans owne brood. Their manner of life is much like to the popish Hermits."[16]

13. Bond, "Source of Knowledge, Source of Power," 119.

14. John Smith, *The Generall Historie of Virginia, New England, and the Summer Isles*, reprinted in Phillip L. Barbour, ed., *The Complete Works of Captain John Smith (1580–1631)*, 3 vols. (Chapel Hill: University of North Carolina Press, 1986) 2:106, 115, 122–23, 149, and 151 (quotation).

15. George Percy, "Observations gathered out of a Discourse of the Plantations of the Southerne Colonie in Virginia by the English, 1606," in *Narratives of Early Virginia, 1606–1625*, ed. Lyon Gardiner Tyler (New York: Barnes & Noble, 1952) 12.

16. Alexander Whitaker, *Good Newes from Virginia*, ed. Wesley Frank Craven (1613; reprint, New York: Scholars' Facsimiles & Reprints, 1937) 24, 26; see also Bond, "Source of Knowledge, Source of Power," 120–25, and Alexander Whitaker to William Crashaw, 9 August 1611, in *Genesis of the United States: A Narrative of the Movement in England, 1605–1616*, ed. Alexander Brown, 49 (New York: Russell & Russell, 1964).

And while they never used the word English settlers readily implied the charge of priestcraft. William Strachey made the clearest comparison in the literature of early Virginia. He envisioned a simple Native "laytie" under the control of powerful priests and conjurers: "(so much are the people at Priests devotion) [they] are ready to execute any thing (how desperate soever which they shall Comaund)."[17] The Reverend Jonas Stockam hinted at a corrupt and manipulative priesthood as well when he discussed what he believed was the chief deterrent to Christianizing Virginia's Native population: "till their Priests and Ancients have their throats cut, there is no hope to bring them to conversion."[18]

Native culture presented a profound threat to English missionary efforts, for many English people did not think of human nature as a fixed quality. It was malleable and could change depending on the particular cultural and environmental setting in which an individual lived. Robert Gray, a supporter of the Virginia venture, articulated this position, one that was at the same time both hopeful and threatening: "it is not the nature of men, but the education of men, which makes them barbarous and uncivill, and therefore chaunge the education of men, and you shall see that their nature will be greatly rectified."[19] William Crashaw made a similar point when he wrote that with a "strict forme of government, and severe discipline [individuals] . . . doe often become new men, even as it were cast in a good mould."[20] If human nature was not a fixed quality, then civility and savagery were not absolute categories either, but unstable forms of existence intimately related to cultural environment. This was all the more frightening to English settlers because Native culture was embraced by men and women like themselves "that with vs (infallibly) they had one, and the same discent and begynning from the vniversall Deluge, in the scattering of Noah his children and Nephewes."[21] Nonetheless, the English saw Native Americans as potential converts because they believed

---

17. Strachey, *Travell into Virginia*, 95, 89.

18. Smith, *Generall Historie*, in Barbour, ed., *Complete Works of Captain John Smith*, 2:286.

19. Gray, *Good Speed to Virginia*, C-2.

20. Crashaw, *Sermon Preached in London*, F-1.

21. Strachey, *Travell into Virginia*, 53; see also Kupperman, *Settling with the Indians*, 106, 118–19.

in the universality of Christianity, and believed that anyone could convert and become Christian.[22]

As a result, efforts to convert Native Americans to Christianity, based on the twin premises of the malleability of human nature and the power of education, were marked by an extreme wariness. The English missionary impulse, limited as it was in Virginia, kept Native peoples at a distance, reflecting a defensive effort designed to protect English settlers from a dangerous foreign culture. Unlike Jesuits in New France or Maryland who traveled among the indigenous populations to win converts, sometimes adopting their ways of life, English missionary efforts in Virginia and New England attempted to "allure" Natives to colonial society through a process that might be called "cultural evangelism." The process was one in which English communities in Virginia embracing "peace and love as becometh xpians" would demonstrate the gentle Christian life, and the Natives, observing this style of living and being impressed by it, would forsake their own culture and ask to become both English and Christian.[23]

## CHANGING STRATEGIES FOR CHRISTIAN MISSION TO NATIVE AMERICANS

By 1609, however, the Virginia Company began to question how successful the settlers at Jamestown might be at attracting adult Native Americans to English society and suggested a change in tactics. The Company's instructions to Sir Thomas Gates implied that winning Natives to Christianity might best be advanced by removing Native children from their own cultural environment and raising them as English people. In Jamestown they could learn "yor language and manners" in a proper English cultural setting.[24] Still young and apparently more malleable than their parents,

22. Rebecca Anne Goetz, "From Potential Christians to Hereditary Heathens: Religion and Race in the Early Chesapeake, 1590–1740" (PhD diss., Harvard University, 2006).

23. Susan Myra Kingsbury, ed., "Instructions to Thomas West Knight Lo: La Warr, 1609/10?," in *The Records of the Virginia Company of London*, 4 vols. (Washington, DC: Government Printing Office, 1906–1935) 3.26 (question mark attached to title in the Kingsbury edition). See also John Frederick Woolverton, *Colonial Anglicanism in North America* (Detroit: Wayne State University Press, 1985) 38–39, 59–67; Bernard W. Sheehan, *Savagism and Civility: Indians and Englishmen in Colonial North America* (Cambridge: Cambridge University Press, 1980) 125–26; Kupperman, *Settling with the Indians*, 164–65.

24. Instructions to Sir Thomas Gates, in Kingsbury, ed., *Records of the Virginia Company of London*, 3:14.

"theire minds not overgrowne with evill Customes" that they no longer questioned, Native children could more easily be prepared for potential conversion to Christianity.[25] By immersion in English culture, which offered a visual feast of educational possibilities, Native children could become civil, then move on and complete the transformation of their natures by becoming Christians.

English Protestants in Virginia tended to associate Christianity with English culture, positing a hostile relationship between Christian and "heathen" ways. Religion to them did not seem to shape culture as much as culture shaped religion, and English culture provided the setting in which true Christianity might take root. One author even linked the transformative power of divine grace, perhaps its very existence, to English culture: "concerning the baptisme of Infidelle children . . . after the manner of primitive guerre, such as mak servants or bondmen to Christians, and more xpetially to remane among them might be baptized."[26]

Colonial authorities recognized the power of Native American culture because they believed they had seen how it had transformed settlers whose work as translators for the settlement forced them to spend long periods of time among the Natives. Living as they did on the margins of English and Native American society, these men were often described as men "that had in [them] more of the Savage then of the Christian" or had "in a manner turned heathen."[27] Only language betrayed the cultural origins of one Englishman who had spent several years among the Natives. In every other way he had been transformed. According to Ralph Hamor, he had become "both in complexion and habit like a salvage."[28] Living

25. Treasurer and Council for Virginia to the Governor and Council in Virginia, 1 August 1622, in *Records of the Virginia Company of London*, ed. Kingsbury, 3:672; Edmund S. Morgan, *American Slavery, American Freedom: The Ordeal of Colonial Virginia* (New York: Norton, 1976) 47, 98.

26. Richard Ferrar to [George Thorpe], 13 December 1618, Ferrar Papers, 93, Magdalene College, Cambridge University, Virginia Colonial Records Project (hereafter cited as VCRP) The VCRP is available at The Virginia Historical Society, The Library of Virginia, the Earl Gregg Swem Library at the College of William and Mary, and the special collections library at the University of Virginia.

27. H. R. McIlwaine, ed., *Journals of the House of Burgesses of Virginia, 1619–1658/1659* (Richmond, VA: Colonial/Waddey, 1915) 15.

28. Quoted in Nicholas Canny, "The Permissive Frontier: Social Control in English Settlements in Ireland and Virginia, 1550–1650," in *The Westward Enterprise: English Activities in Ireland, the Atlantic and America, 1480–1650*, ed. K. R. Andrews, N. P. Canny, and P. E. H. Hair (Detroit: Wayne State University Press, 1979) 32.

outside English society, cut off from their traditional cultural institutions, the natures of English settlers could change; they could cross the divide and become "savage" themselves. The Reverend John Brinsley suggested that Native culture held the same power to change human nature. Native American culture, he argued, presented "manifold perils . . . especially of falling away from God to Sathan, and that themselves, or their [English] posterity should become utterly savage, as they [Natives] are."[29] Nor were Natives ignorant of this cultural competition. "In their own villages," according to historian Bernard Sheehan, Native Americans were in fact "ardent proselytizers" of captured Europeans.[30]

The leaders of the Virginia Company consistently emphasized the importance of trying to spread the Gospel to Virginia's indigenous people. Yet, this missionary zeal was not necessarily embraced by Jamestown's settlers. George Thorpe summed up the settlers attitudes in 1621 when he wrote, "There is scarce any man amongst us that doth afforde [the Natives] a good thought in his hart and most men with their mouthes give them nothinge but maledictions and bitter execrations."[31] Thorpe and John Pory worried that God's judgment would soon be visited upon the colony for "wee doe not as wee ought to doe, take his service a long wth us by o[u]r serious endevours of convertinge the Heathens."[32] They were a vast minority, however. Colonists even diverted funds donated by pious supporters in England intended to further missionary efforts at the College of Henrico to another purpose, financing an iron mill.[33] Colonists did not want Native children in their midst learning civility and Christianity—too much prejudice, too much bother, yet another task that might keep them from cultivating tobacco. And the vast majority of Native Americans in Virginia were unimpressed with the English gift of Christianity. Following the Powhatan uprising in 1622 what mission to

---

29. John Brinsley, *The Consolation of Our Grammar Schools* . . . (London, 1622) A2–A3.

30. Sheehan, *Savigism and Civility*, 110–13, quotation on 113.

31. George Thorpe and John Pory to Edwin Sandys, 15 and 16 May 1621, in Kingsbury, ed., *The Records of the Virginia Company of London*, 3:446.

32. Ibid.

33. Charles E. Hatch Jr. and Thurlow Gates Gregory, "The First American Blast Furnace, 1619–1622: The Birth of a Mighty Industry on Falling Creek in Virginia," in *Virginia Magazine of History and Biography* 70 (1962) 267–68.

the Natives had existed collapsed, replaced by calls for the eradication of the Natives from "being any longer a people."[34]

Nearly seventy years passed before Commissary James Blair attempted to establish another mission to Virginia's indigenous peoples, suggesting in his proposal to establish a college in Virginia that one of the institution's goals would be to ensure "that the Christian Faith may be propagated amongst the Western *Indians*."[35] Blair also had the good fortune to secure for the new college a sizable portion of Sir Robert Boyle's "Legacy for pious uses" left by the scientist at his death in 1691. The commissary intended to have the College of William and Mary use the bequest for the purpose of converting Native Americans to Christianity. Few Natives, however, were interested. In 1697 when the Boyle funds were officially transferred to the College, a school existed but no Indians were yet enrolled—and there was little hope of finding Native Americans willing to attend the school. Virginia Indians refused to send their children to the college, in part because they believed that children sent there to receive an education had been sold as slaves. Many of the Native Americans who later did attend William and Mary were captives from remote tribes who had been purchased from local Natives.[36] Writing in the same year to the Board of Trade, Governor Edmund Andros responded to a query about Virginians' efforts to spread the Gospel to the Natives with an answer that likely contained more truth than hyperbole: "None ever heard of."[37]

The efforts by Blair and others to educate and convert Native children at William and Mary followed the same pattern established years earlier by the Virginia Company of London—becoming Christian demanded removal from Native society. They would become Christians at the college not within their own societies.

Lieutenant Governor Alexander Spotswood was likely the political figure in seventeenth and eighteenth-century Virginia most interested in missionary work among the colony's Native peoples. During his tenure, in fact, Indian enrollment at William and Mary reached its peak. In ad-

34. Bond, "Source of Knowledge, Source of Power," 136.

35. Michael Anesko, "So Discreet a Zeal: Slavery and the Anglican Church in Virginia, 1680–1730," *Virginia Magazine of History and Biography* 93 (1985) 258–59.

36. Ibid., 268–69.

37. W. Stitt Robinson Jr., "Indian Education and Missions in Colonial Virginia," *Journal of Southern History* 18 (1952) 152–68, Andros quotation on 161.

dition, Spotwood established a school for tributary Indians dedicated to the twin goals of education and Christianization at Christanna on the south side of the Meherrin River and paid the schoolmaster from his own funds. Unlike education at the college, Natives at Spotswood school remained free and close to their families. The act that established the school, however, also gave the Virginia Indian Company a monopoly on trade with local Natives and drew intense opposition as a result. Ultimately the crown disallowed the law in 1717.[38]

With his plans for the school at Christanna in disarray, Spotswood turned his efforts at educating and Christianizing Virginia's Native peoples to William and Mary. Alas, the Indian School was already in decline. In 1723 college leaders did use the Boyle funds to construct a building for the Indian School; within a decade it also came to house the college's library. The school never fulfilled its purpose of training Native men so that they could "be sent abroad to preach and convert the Indians."[39] Most English Virginians cared about neither the Natives' salvation nor their education. Nor did the Natives care for being cooped up in a school building where they learned skills they considered useless. The Iroquois once reflected on the deficiencies of their young people educated at the college, complaining that they "were absolutely good for nothing being neither acquainted with the true methods for killing deer, catching Beaver or surprizing an enemy."[40] One student of Indian education at William and Mary concluded that the school's efforts "brought little credit to the College, and less accomplishment."[41]

The best work on this subject, Rebecca Goetz's, suggests that by the end of the seventeenth century English Virginians had largely given up on their efforts to convert Native Americans to Christianity. "Anglo-Virginians," Goetz argues, "had successfully engineered religious belief and membership in the Christian community into a racial ideology that connected the physical and cultural differences the English attributed to Indians and Africans with an idea of permanent spiritual inferiority." In

38. Margaret Connell Szasz, *Indian Education in the American Colonies, 1607–1783* (Albuquerque: University of New Mexico Press, 1988) 69–74; Anesko, "So Discreet a Zeal," 273–76.

39. Szasz, *Indian Education in the American Colonies*, 77.

40. Ibid.

41. Karen A. Stuart, "'So Good a Work': The Brafferton School, 1691–1777" (MA thesis, College of William and Mary, 1984) 70, 81.

short, Native Americans and Africans had moved from "potential converts" to "hereditary heathens" beyond the Christian pale.[42]

## CHRISTIAN MISSION AND AFRICAN SLAVES IN COLONIAL VIRGINIA

While white Virginians could easily avoid the issue of Christianizing Native Americans since the two groups lived in different societies, they could not as readily avoid the issue of spreading the Gospel to African and African American slaves who lived within English Virginia. In fact, as residents within Virginia parishes, they were technically part of the colony's established church. The sources as well as the historiography suggest ambiguous conclusions about both the seriousness and the success of Virginians' efforts to Christianize slaves. In addition, the efforts of Anglican and dissenting ministers to spread the Gospel among the colony's black population resulted in unintended consequences that served to strengthen the institution of slavery. The topic is complex, not only because planters and pastors often disagreed about evangelism in the slave quarters, but also because African and African American attitudes toward Christianity changed over the course of nearly two hundred years. Many of the first generation of Africans brought to the colony and their first generation African American descendants professed the religion of Christ crucified. Ira Berlin has described the first generation of Africans in Virginia—slave, indentured, and free—as "Atlantic creoles," people who "understood the languages of the Atlantic, bore Hispanic and occasionally English names, and were familiar with Christianity and other aspects of European culture," especially its laws.[43] Between 1619, the latest date when Africans were first brought to North America, and the late 1660s, there is evidence black men and women attended the colony's established church, had their children baptized, and did penance alongside white Virginians during divine service. Enslaved creoles like Elizabeth Key aware that English custom and law denied Christians the right to hold other Christians as slaves sued for their freedom in the colony's courts

42. Goetz, "From Potential Christians to Hereditary Heathens" (see n. 22 above). The quotation derives from a preliminary draft of Goetz's dissertation, which page number I have not provided as the pagination differs from that in the approved and bound version.

43. Ira Berlin, *Many Thousands Gone: The First Two Centuries of Slavery in North America* (Cambridge: Harvard University Press, 1998) 17–46.

and sometimes won their way out of bondage.[44] (Annette Laing has argued persuasively that African slaves brought to South Carolina from the Kongo, many of whom had been exposed to Roman Catholicism, actively sought out liturgical religion like that practiced by the Church of England.[45])

Attitudes began to change, however, during the 1660s. Virginia's General Assembly passed a law establishing and defining chattel slavery and later in the decade, in 1667, passed a statute denying the traditional correspondence of Christianity with freedom. It declared that "baptisme doth not alter the condition of the person as to his bondage or ffreedome," a position reaffirmed in 1727 in a series of pastoral letters written by Edmund Gibson, bishop of London.[46] One of the founders of the Society for the Propagation of the Gospel in Foreign Parts, William Fleetwood, emphasized in his 1701 work, *The Relative Duties of Parents ad Children, Husbands and Wives, Masters and Servants,* that God had created a hierarchical world and baptism did not change those hierarchical relationships and stations.[47] Virginians, however, seemed reluctant to accept this position, instead continuing in many cases to associate Christianity with freedom. The first extant source outlining the conflict in Virginia between planters and parsons over efforts to Christianize slaves also dates to the 1660s. Morgan Godwyn, a young Oxford graduate inspired by Bede's

44. Warren M. Billings, "The Cases of Fernando and Elizabeth Key: A Note on the Status of Blacks in Seventeenth-Century Virginia," *William and Mary Quarterly* 3rd ser. 30 (1973) 469–71. See also, Rebecca A. Goetz, "'The Child Should be Made a Christian': Baptism, Race, and Identity in the Early Chesapeake," in *Race and Identity in the New World,* ed. John Garrigus (College Station: Texas A. & M. Press, forthcoming).

45. Annette Laing, "'Heathens and Infidels'? African Christianization and Anglicanism in the South Carolina Low Country, 1700–1750," in *Religion and American Culture* 12 (2002) 197–228. See also Nicholas M. Beasley, "Domestic Rituals: Marriage and Baptism in the British Plantation Colonies, 1650–1780," in *Anglican and Episcopal History* 76 (2007) 327–57, and Philip D. Morgan, *Slave Counterpoint: Black Culture in the Eighteenth-Century Chesapeake and Lowcountry* (Chapel Hill: University of North Carolina Press, 1998) 1–21.

46. William Waller Hening, comp., *The Statutes at Large: Being a Collection of All the Laws of Virginia,* 13 vols. (Richmond, 1809–1823) 2:260; Edmund Gibson, *Two Letters of the Lord Bishop of London* (London, 1728; 2nd ed., 1729) 21–22. Perhaps the best discussion of Gibson's position may be found in Sylvia R. Frey and Betty Wood, *Come Shouting to Zion: African American Protestantism in the American South and British Caribbean to 1830* (Chapel Hill: University of North Carolina Press, 1998) 68–70.

47. Charles F. Irons, *The Origins of Proslavery Christianity: White and Black Evangelicals in Colonial Virginia* (Chapel Hill: University of North Carolina Press, 2008) 30.

*Ecclesiastical History of the English Nation* and its saga of how the Romans had brought Christianity to the motley tribe of ancient Britons, arrived in Virginia in 1665 ready to act upon the Great Commission and spread the Gospel among the colony's slave population. (Godwyn, in fact, anticipated the attitude of an eighteenth-century Anglican minister in Virginia, the Rev. Jonathan Boucher, who wrote: "Negroes when compared with any other class of people in a Christian country, are no doubt lamentably ignorant; yet I saw no reason to think they were more so than many of the first converts to Christianity must needs have been."[48]) Colonists, however, balked at Godwyn's efforts to convert their slaves. One woman went so far as to suggest that if Godwyn insisted upon baptizing slaves he should go ahead and sprinkle water on "her black Bitch" for all the good it would do.[49]

Baptism acknowledged both a common humanity and the potential freedom of the individual, something Virginians did not wish to admit about their slaves, regardless of a received English tradition that argued for the incompatibility of slavery and Christianity. As a willfully chosen faith identity Christianity transcended race and cultural identity, the invisible and indelible marks of grace obliterating temporal appearances, with freedom one of its earthly benefits. Governor William Berkeley acted on this equation in the 1660s when he offered three Turkish slaves both freedom and plantations if they would convert to Christianity.[50]

As a result of the law regarding baptism the blurred racial lines of the first half of the century identified by Ira Berlin became fixed and rigid. Christianity then became the basis of a white cultural identity, a possession in the minds of many Virginians proper to white people alone. "These two words," Godwyn wrote, "Negro and Slave, being by custom grown Homogeneous and Convertible; even as *Negro* and *Christian, Englishman* and *Heathen,* are by the like corrupt Custom and Partiality made *Opposites*; thereby as if implying that the one could not be *Christians,* nor the other *Infidels.*"[51] Linking cultural identity with religious faith prescribed the

---

48. Boucher quoted in John K. Nelson, *A Blessed Company: Parishes, Parsons, and Parishioners in Anglican Virginia, 1690-1776* (Chapel Hill: University of North Carolina Press, 2001) 266.

49. Woolverton, *Colonial Anglicanism in North America,* 71–72.

50. John Clayton, *The Defence of a Sermon, Preach'd upon the Receiving into the Communion of the Church of England* (Dublin, 1701), preface, no pagination.

51. Morgan Godwyn, *The Negro's and Indian's Advocate Suing for their Admission into the Church* (London, 1680) 36.

world white planters wanted to exist. Commissary James Blair later noted the existence in the colony of white individuals he called "Christians by birth" rather than choice.[52] As his phrase suggests, individuals inherited their identity at birth, and as a purveyor of meaning the cultural inheritance meant more than the faith. As historian Charles Irons has pointed out:"Anglicans in Virginia who accepted this religious distinction between slave and free could not make the imaginative leap of including people of color in the body of Christ."[53]

Black attitudes toward Christianity also began to change in the latter decades of the seventeenth century. With the success of the "planter revolution" and with chattel slavery recognized in law, planters turned with greater frequency to African slaves rather than white indentured servants to meet their increasing need for laborers. As the demand for slaves increased, the source of those slaves also changed. The majority of slaves imported to the colony no longer came from the Atlantic littoral; instead they came from the interior of the African continent. Unlike the Chesapeake's charter generation, later generations of slaves imported to the colony were often strangers to Christianity and European culture. By 1700, Africans from the interior of the continent "comprised nearly 90 percent of the slave population" in the colony.[54]

Changes that began in the 1660s set the terms of the debate over evangelizing slaves for over a century. Ministers and masters willing to allow proselytizing complained that the mutual incomprehension of slaves recently arrived from Africa and English missionaries presented insurmountable obstacles to conversion, a complaint made by Presbyterians and Quakers as well as by Anglicans.[55] Many Virginians, in fact, only reluctantly accepted the 1667 law about baptism and, as a result, efforts to spread the Gospel into the slave quarters lagged. The equation of freedom with Christianity continued to shape the perceptions of many slavehold-

52. James Blair, *Our Saviour's Divine Sermon on the Mount, Contain'd in the Vth, VIth, and VIIIth chapters of St. Matthew's Gospel, Explained; and the Practice of it Recommended in divers Sermons and Discourses*, 5 vols. (London, 1722) 3.282.

53. Irons, *Origins of Proslavery Christianity*, 25.

54. Berlin, *Many Thousands Gone*, 109–12, quotation on 110.

55. Rev. James Marye Jr. to Rev. John Waring, 25 September 1764, in John C. Van Horne, ed., *Religious Philanthropy and Colonial Slavery: The American Correspondence of the Associates of Dr. Bray, 1717–1777* (Urbana: University of Illinois Press, 1985) 219; Epistles Received, vol. 4 (1759–1778) 56, Library of the Society of Friends, London, VCRP.

ers. The effect Christianity would have on slaves often led to proclamations that might tell us more about the authors' understanding of human nature than of the relationship between Christianity and slavery. Some colonists complained that baptism made slaves "prouder," while others believed it filled their bondsmen with unfounded "thoughts of freedom."[56] The large number of Africans unfamiliar with both the English language and the Christian religion made some people suspect the sincerity of slave conversions, that they were but a ruse to gain freedom. James Blair mused: "I doubt not some of the Negroes are sincere Converts; but the far greater part of them little mind the serious part, only are in hopes that they shall meet with so much more respect, and that some time or other Christianity will help them to their freedom."[57] Lieutenant Governor William Gooch, in fact, blamed a threatened slave rebellion in 1730 on a rumor that "his Majesty had sent Orders for setting of them free as soon as they were Christians, and that these Orders were suppressed."[58] In order both to prevent slaves from expecting baptism to free them from bondage and to allay planter fears that they did, Francis Le Jau of South Carolina added to the baptismal service language that each slave seeking baptism had to agree to: "You declare in the Presence of God and before this Congregation that you do not ask for the holy baptism out of any design to ffree [sic] yourself from the Duty and Obedience you owe to your Master while you live, but merely for the good of Your Soul and to partake of the Grace and Blessing promised to members of the Church of Jesus Christ."[59]

Ministers who did attempt to convert slaves often met with great resistance. The Reverend John Bagg of St. Anne's Parish claimed that his parishioners were "generally not approving thereof, being led away by the notion of their [slaves] being and becoming worse slaves when

56. Hugh Jones, *The Present State of Virginia, From Whence is Inferred a Short View of Maryland and North Carolina* (London, 1724), ed. Richard Morton (Chapel Hill: University of North Carolina Press, 1956) 99; James Blair to Bishop Gibson, 20 July 1730, Fulham Palace Papers, vol. 13, no. 131, Lambeth Palace Library, VCRP.

57. James Blair to Bishop Gibson, 28 June 1729, Fulham Palace Papers, vol. 15, no. 109, VCRP.

58. Public Records Office, Colonial Office, 5/1322, Part I, 158, VCRP.

59. Nicholas M. Beasley, *Christian Ritual and the Creation of British Slave Societies, 1650-1789* (Athens: University of Georgia Press, 2009) 76.

Christians."[60] Other people objected to being in the presence of blacks at church and refused to attend integrated services, especially baptisms. The Reverend Alexander Rhonnald of Elizabeth River Parish in Norfolk County demonstrated too great a missionary zeal to suit the taste of many slaveholders in his parish. He complained: "They use Me with the most invidious Terms of ill nature for my pains, & because I baptize more Negroes than other Brethren here & instruct them from the Pulpit, out of common road, & encourage the Good among them to come to the Communion, after a due Sense of the matter, I am vilified & branded by such as a Negro Parson."[61] James Maury, Andrew White, James Marye, and Adam Dickie, whose life was threatened, all ran into trouble with their parishioners for performing integrated baptisms.[62] Between 1700 and his death in 1743, Commissary James Blair, according to some historians, hindered efforts to spread Christianity to slaves. Much of his power rested upon alliances he had established through marriage and expediency with members of Virginia's ruling elite; to attack Virginians' reluctance to baptize their slaves was therefore to attack his patrons.[63] Conversely, the Rev. William Willie of Albemarle Parish baptized over one thousand slave children in the four decades before the American Revolution, and the Rev. Thomas Baker of Kingston Parish claimed in 1770 that slaves approached him every Sunday asking that he baptize them or their children, evidence perhaps of both the spread of Christianity into the slaves quarters and a changing African and African American attitude toward Christianity.[64]

Nonetheless, numerous clergymen continued to press the issue. The methods they relied on reflected those used to prepare unbaptized white people to receive the sacrament of baptism. The Presbyterian Samuel Davies and Anglican Jonathan Boucher, for example, were among the ministers who attempted to teach slaves to read and distributed religious tracts to those who were literate. Boucher's practice may have been typical: "I have already distributed many of [the books] amongst the poor Slaves who are very numerous in this Parish. In many of my former let-

60. The Rev. John Bagg, response to queries from the bishop of London, Fulham Palace Papers, vol. 12, 41–44, VCRP.

61. The Rev. Alexander Rhonnald to the Rev. John Waring, 27 September 1762, in Van Horne, ed., *Religious Philanthropy and Colonial Slavery*, 181.

62. Gundersen, *Anglican Ministry in Virginia*, 111–12.

63. Anesko, "So Discreet a Zeal," 252–53, 278.

64. Nelson, *Blessed Company*, 266–67.

ters I have told You of the Difficulties Ministers are under to reconcile Owners of Slaves to their being instructed. . . . I generally find an old Negro, or a conscientious Overseer, able to read, whom I give Books, with an Injunction to Them to instruct such & such Slaves in their respective Neighbourhoods."[65] During the penitential season of Lent in the 1740s, the Reverend William Dawson organized public readings of devotional literature at the College of William and Mary. At these gatherings upperclassmen read religious tracts aloud to groups comprised of lowerclassmen, slaves, Native Americans, and indentured servants.[66]

Anglican ministers were supported in their efforts to spread the message of the Gospel to Virginia's slave population by the Associates of Dr. Bray, a group formed in 1723/24 to help educate and Christianize blacks in the colonies. The Associates sent books to colonial ministers for this purpose and established schools for blacks in Philadelphia (1758), New York (1760), Williamsburg (1760), Newport, Rhode Island (1762), and Fredericksburg, Virginia (1765). The Williamsburg school had a successful run of fourteen years, closing in 1774 after the death of its teacher. The Fredericksburg school proved less successful. The town's small population was unable to sustain the experiment and the school closed in 1770.[67]

Despite a great deal of planter resistance, some ministers were able to teach some slaves about Christianity. In an extraordinary letter written to the bishop of London in 1723 by an anonymous Virginia slave—who had either read the Bible or heard the Exodus story—the writer complained that "wee are commandded to keep holey the Sabbath day and wee doo hardly know when it comes for our task mastrs are as hard with us as the Egpttions was with the Chilldann of Issarell." The writer also knew the requirements for baptism, requesting that the bishop "Settell one thing upon us which is that our childarn may be broatt up in the way of the Christtian faith and our desire is that they may be Larnd the Lords prayer

---

65. The Rev. Jonathan Boucher to the Rev. Waring, 9 March 1767, in Van Horne, ed., *Religious Philanthropy and Colonial Slavery*, 255; George William Pilcher, *Samuel Davies: Apostle of Dissent in Colonial Virginia* (Knoxville: University of Tennessee Press, 1971) 105.

66. William Dawson to Dr. Bearcroft, 12 July 1744, Dawson Papers, 1:22, Library of Congress.

67. Van Horne, ed., *Religious Philanthropy and Colonial Slavery*, 6–7, 20–25; Gundersen, *Anglican Ministry in Virginia*, 114–15.

the creed and the ten commandments and that they may appeare Every Lord's day att Church."[68]

In all likelihood, attempts to evangelize slaves were as individual as the relationships among particular slaves, particular masters, and particular ministers. Some masters took the duty more seriously than others, just as some slaves no doubt desired to become Christians more than others and just as some ministers pressed the work more vigorously than others. Ministers' complaints about slave owners who did not want their slaves to become Christians must be balanced against other evidence that suggests that slaves were expected to gain at least nominal exposure to the teachings of the church. Some Virginia churches, for instance, contained slave galleries, implying that slaves would attend worship services. Philip Vickers Fithian (1747–1776), a tutor employed by Robert Carter of Nomini Hall in 1773 and 1774, described the whole parish meeting together on Sundays, "High, Low, black, white."[69] Another tutor, the indentured servant John Harrower (ca. 1734–1777), recorded in his journal the baptisms of slave infants born on William Daingerfield's plantation and noted as well that one of his own tasks was to teach the catechism to slave children when they reached the appropriate age.[70] And despite the trouble he ran into for holding integrated baptisms, the Reverend Adam Dickie of Drysdale Parish suggested that many slave owners detected a worthwhile change in their slaves' behavior after they had received catechetical training: bondsmen "who formerly were thieves, lyars, Swearers, prophaners of the Sabbath, and neglecters of their business, from a Sense of Religion and of their Duty have left off all these things."[71] Readers should also keep in mind that many ministers owned slaves themselves.[72] They attacked not

68. Thomas N. Ingersoll, "'Release us out of this Cruell Bondegg': An Appeal from Virginia in 1723," in *William and Mary Quarterly* 3rd ser. 51 (1994) 781–82.

69. Hunter Dickinson Farish, ed., *Journal & Letters of Philip Vickers Fithian, 1773–1774: A Planter Tutor in the Old Dominion* (Williamsburg, VA: Colonial Williamsburg Society, 1965) 89. For the most recent biography of Fithian, see John Fea, *The Way of Enlightenment Leads Home: Philip Vickers Fithian and the Rural Enlightenment in Early America* (Philadelphia: University of Pennsylvania Press, 2008).

70. Edward Miles Riley, ed., *The Journal of John Harrower, an Indentured Servant in the Colony of Virginia, 1773–1776* (Williamsburg, VA: Colonial Williamsburg Society, 1963) xviii, 48, 124.

71. Nelson, *Blessed Company*, 259–73, quotation on 264.

72. The Reverend Anthony Gavin provides a rare example of a colonial minister in Virginia who openly opposed the institution of slavery. See Anthony Gavin to Bishop

the institution itself but the lack of charity on the part of slave masters who prevented their slaves from hearing the message of salvation contained in the Gospel.

## CONCLUSION

In the thirty or so years before and after the American Revolution the equation between heathen and African began to fade, in large part after the war as a result of slaves joining evangelical churches or starting their own when whites refused them membership or moved too slowly to let them join. While some white evangelicals challenged the institution of slavery, in the long run proslavery Christianity (the roots of which stretched back to Godwyn, Fleetwood, Samuel Davies, and the numerous Anglican and dissenting clergy who sought to convert slaves by arguing that Christianity would make them better slaves) became dominant in Virginia by 1800.[73] And with it, the paternalism of the colonial period

---

Gibson, 5 August 1738, Fulham Palace Papers, vol. 14, no. 151, VCRP: "it gives me great deal of uneasines to see the greatest Part of our Brethren taken up in farming and buying Slaves, which in my humble Opinion is unlawfull for any Christian, and particularly for a Clergyman, by this the Souls Committed to their Care must suffer." For more on Gavin, see Joan R. Gundersen, "Anthony Gavin's *A Master-key to Popery:* A Virginia Parson's Best Seller," *Virginia Magazine of History and Biography* 82 (1974) 39–46.

73. Irons, *Origins of Proslavery Christianity*, 61–63. See also, Randolph Ferguson Scully, *Religion and the Making of Nat Turner's Virginia: Baptist Community and Conflict, 1740–1840* (Charlottesville: University of Virginia Press, 2008). The literature on efforts to spread the Gospel among slaves in the Antebellum South is immense. See, e.g., John B. Boles, ed., *Masters and Slaves in the House of the Lord: Race and Religion in the American South, 1740–1870* (Lexington: University of Kentucky Press, 1988), and Janet Duitsman Cornelius, *Slave Missions and the Black Church in the Antebellum South* (Columbia: University of South Carolina Press, 1999). On slave religion, see Albert J. Raboteau, *Slave Religion: The "Invisible Institution" in the Antebellum South* (New York: Oxford University Press, 1978).

I am most familiar with the Episcopal Church and its efforts to Christianize slaves. On this topic, see the work of Nicholas M. Beasley (cited above, nn. 45 and 59); J. Carleton Hayden, "Conversion and Control: Dilemma of Episcopalians in Providing for the Religious Instruction of Slaves, Charleston, South Carolina, 1845–1860," in *Historical Magazine of the Protestant Episcopal Church* 40 (1971) 143–72; S. C. Bolton, "South Carolina and the Reverend Doctor Francis Le Jau: Southern Society and the Conscience of an Anglican Missionary," in *Historical Magazine of the Protestant Episcopal Church* 40 (1971) 63–80; N. Brooks Graebner, "The Episcopal Church and Race in Nineteenth Century North Carolina," in *Anglican and Episcopal History* 78 (2009) 84–93; and Edward L. Bond, "Slavery in the Diocese of Mississippi's Conventions Journals, 1826–1861," in *Anglican and Episcopal History* 78 (2009) 94–104. For a broader history of African

continued. Granted, in some cases, Sunday Schools taught slaves to read, sometimes even after laws banning the practice had been passed,[74] but in general white Christians continued to see African American and Native Americans as people in need of civilizing and white leadership, an attitude that would continue into the twentieth century.[75]

---

Americans and the Episcopal Church, see Harold T. Lewis, *Yet with a Steady Beat: The African American Struggle for Recognition in the Episcopal Church* (Valley Forge, PA: Trinity, 1996).

74. Edward L. Bond and Joan R. Gundersen, "The Episcopal Church in Virginia, 1607–2007," *Virginia Magazine of History and Biography* 115 (2007) 228.

75. I would like to thank the editor of the *Virginia Magazine of History and Biography* and the editors at Mercer University Press for allowing me to reproduce here portions of my "Source of Knowledge, Source of Power: The Supernatural World of English Virginia, 1607–1624," *Virginia Magazine of History and Biography* 108 (2000) 153–88; "The Religion of Anglicans in James Blair's Virginia: Private Piety in the Public Church, 1685–1743," *Virginia Magazine of History and Biography* 104 (1996) 313–40; and *Damned Souls in a Tobacco Colony: Religion in Seventeenth-Century Virginia* (Macon, GA: Mercer University Press, 2000).

# PART THREE

# Re-Engaging the Christian Mission to Native America

5

# Living in Transition, Embracing Community, and Envisioning God's Mission as Trinitarian Mutuality

*Reflections from a Native-American Follower of Jesus*

RICHARD TWISS

*Christian mission among the tribes of North America has not been very good news. What worldview influences allowed the Creator's story of creation and redemption to morph into a hegemonic colonial myth justifying the genocide and exploitation of America's First Nations people? What can be done to deconstruct that myth and move its focus away from a Eurocentric core? We will explore perspectives from North American Indigenous theologians and their experiences as participants within that story that might help reorient it to a biblical narrative that pursues a redemptive community in/through diversity.*

## INTRODUCTION

THE MORE I READ about the period of missionary history surrounding the Jamestown era I became as disillusioned and skeptical as ever about Christianity and missionary endeavors among our First Nations people.

It was a defining moment in my journey as a Lakota follower of Jesus when Jerry Yellowhawk prayed over me in a Lakota naming ceremony, giving me the name *Taoyate Obnajin* "He Stands With His People," and Vincent Yellow Old Woman gifted me with his eagle feather war bonnet to confirm the name and Creator's gifting in my life.

My father is Oglala Lakota/Sioux from the Pine Ridge Reservation and my mother is Sicangu Lakota/Sioux from the Rosebud Reservation, both in South Dakota. I was born and lived among my mother's people until age 6, when we moved away from the reservation. I grew up in a small town in Oregon from grades 3–12 then moved back to Rosebud to attend Sinte Gleska University.

In 1972, along with 600 others, I participated in the American Indian Movement's (AIM) forced takeover and occupation of the Bureau of Indian Affairs Office Building in Washington, DC, protesting the U.S. Federal Government's breaking of more than 700 congressionally ratified treaties that it made with tribes in the United States. During this period of my life I began to allow hatred toward white people and Christianity to grow in my heart. In 1974, however, after years of many painful experiences with drug and alcohol abuse, time in jail and a growing despair of my own lostness, I became a follower of Jesus while living in Maui, Hawaii. I had to learn to love white people and become a Christian then.

As the years passed I began to resist the pressure to accept interpretations of the Bible that said "old things had passed away and all things had become white" regarding my following Jesus in the context of my Native cultural ways, music, dance, drumming, ceremony and culture. In reference to my Native culture I was informed the Bible said "touch not the unclean thing," or "come out from among them and be separate," or "what fellowship does light have with darkness." This meant I needed to leave my Indian ways behind me, because I had a new identity in Christ, and it WAS NOT Indian! The Bible was used to demonize just about everything important to our cultural sense of being one with God and creation.

Sadly, the hegemony of the prevailing worldview assumptions of the European immigrants that typified the efforts of the Jamestown missionaries not only lingers today, but has morphed into a distinct evangelical bias against Native culture and ways.

The missionary efforts among the people located on my reservation over the past 150 years still suffer under the weight of that hegemony and this is typical of the current state of the "Native church." The largest town on the Rosebud Reservation is named Mission. This community of 950 people is so named because it was the place where missionary agencies were invited to set up shop. In July of 2008 I led a cross-cultural immersion course for seminary students in Mission. I sent groups of two or three people to visit nine different churches on a Sunday morning in five different communities. Afterward, during a de-brief time, without exception each group commented that they could have been attending any "white" church in "anywhere" USA. There was nothing "Native" about those mission churches except the fact Natives were sitting in the pews. The music, liturgy, language, décor, and style were all Anglo.

That week I drove around the small community and questioned leaders of various church-sponsored short-term missions groups and counted more than 600 workers in the town of Mission alone for that one week. That's not counting short-term workers in any of the other twenty reservation communities, of which there were hundreds (and this does not count Thanksgiving, Christmas and Easter outreaches). This goes on all summer long, year after year, decade after decade and little changes.

A 2008 *New York Times* article reported that males between 15 and 25 on the Rosebud Reservation have the highest incidence of suicide in America. Poverty, alcohol and drug abuse and all the maladies that accompany these things are staggering in magnitude!

## THE LEGACY OF JAMESTOWN LIVES ON.

When my wife and I lived on the Coeur d'Alene Reservation in Northern Idaho in 1996, we did not know of one Native man who regularly attended any of the six evangelical churches, and barely half a dozen women attended. This was true as well for the neighboring Nez Perce and Kalispell Reservations. This fact stood in stark contrast to an amazing revival in this region that occurred prior to an established colonial presence through a Spokane Indian who is known as Spokane Garry. God used Chief Garry as a "messenger" who bore remarkable fruit through his labor among numerous tribes in Washington, Idaho, Oregon and southward.[1]

Chief Garry was a tribal leader, husband, father and advocate for justice and Christian values who, though his own efforts appeared to have no lasting impact and did not bring the White settlers to an understanding of justice, nevertheless did throughout it all remain faithful to Christ.

The residual witness of God, the "natural revelation" of creation found in Romans 1:19, is a powerful force in the history of these tribes. The First Nations people who occupied the Plateau area of Western Montana and Wyoming, Idaho, Eastern Washington and Oregon had been "visited" by

---

1. Much of this information on Chief Spokane Garry is from my book, *One Church, Many Tribes* (Ventura, CA: Regal, 2000).

a prophetic revelation of God's coming. The following historical accounts show how God had prepared the way for Chief Garry, like the Apostle Paul, to become God's chosen servant and a special messenger among his people.

## Yuree-rachen

In 1782 the first "virgin soil" epidemic swept across the American continent—an epidemic of smallpox. During this mysterious sickness, *Yuree-rachen*, Circling Raven, a shaman of the *Sin-ho-man-naish* (the Middle Spokanes) attempted to minister healing to his people, who lived just west of present-day Spokane, Washington. Rather than heal them by his shamanistic practices, however, he lost his son to the disease, and great numbers of the villagers also perished. *Yuree-rachen* suffered a crisis of faith. Disillusioned and angry, he asked his brother, "If the righteous die while evil men live, why should we continue to follow our laws? Let us live like the animals."

His brother persuaded the shaman to maintain his faith awhile longer in their moral law and in the God they called *Quilent-sat-men*, He-Made-Us. He also persuaded him to go to the top of Mount Spokane for four days of prayer and fasting.

At the conclusion of his fast, according to Spokane tradition, *Yuree-rachen* received a vision of men of white skin wearing strange clothes and bearing in their hands leaves bound together. He was told to counsel his people to prepare for these *chipixa* "white skinned ones" and to pay attention to the teaching that came from the leaves bound together.[2]

## Shining Shirt

The Middle Spokanes were not the only tribe to receive such a prophecy. Nor was this type of prophecy, according to researchers, an isolated quirk, a delusion of primitive minds or a tale invented

2. See Bradford Zeb Long and Douglas McMurry, *The Collapse of the Brass Heaven: Rebuilding Our Worldview to Embrace the Power of God* (Grand Rapids: Chosen, 1994) 209–10. On this same page, Long and McMurry say that, "According to anthropologist Leslie Spier, the tribes of the region developed the 'dream dance' (Dr. Spier calls it the 'Prophet Dance') as a religious response to the widespread revival of such prophecy during the eighteenth century"—referring in their footnote to Leslie Spier, *The Prophet Dance in the Northwest and Its Derivatives: The Source of the Ghost Dance* (Menasha: American Anthropological Association, 1935).

later by Christian-influenced reservation Indians. The great cultural hero Shining Shirt, according to ethnologist Harry Holbert Turney-High, prophesied that white people would come from the East one day: according to the legend Shining Shirt was both a chief and Shaman. After he was a grown man and was in charge of his people, a Power made a great revelation. The Power said that there was a Good and Evil One of which the Indian knew but little so far. Yet the time would come when men with fair skins dressed in long black skirts would come and would teach them the truth. These Indians had never heard of a white man at that early a date.

The Black Robes would change the lives of the people in ways of which they but little dreamed. The Power then gave Shining Shirt a talisman of terrific strength. This was a piece of metal inscribed with a cross.

Then he told them that there is a God. His true name was not revealed but he was temporarily called Amotkan, He-who-lives-on-most-high. Shining Shirt then taught them that the Black Robes would give them a new moral law which they should obey. Now the people trusted Shining Shirt and received his teaching.[3]

According to various accounts, in 1825 Governor George Simpson of the northern division of the Hudson Bay Company, with the permission and support of the tribal leaders, took two young Indian boys in their early teens from the Spokane and Middle Spokane and Lower Kootenay head chiefs for the purpose of educating them at a Mission School at Red River, present day Winnipeg, Manitoba, Canada. The boys were called Spokane Garry and Kootenai Pelly.[4]

After four or five years, by differing accounts, Garry and Pelly returned to Ft. Colville in the summer of 1829. After they returned, vast crowds gathered from hundreds of miles around to hear what these two young men might have to say about the Master of life. The anthropologist, Leslie Spier, who has studied the religious life of the Indians of this region, noted that there was a remarkable spread of Christian practices among the tribes of this area and he determined that "the revival must have spread from the Spokane Country about 1830 or a little later."[5] John

---

3. Long and McMurry, *Collapse of the Brass Heaven*, 210–11.

4. Ibid., 212.

5. Spier, *The Prophet Dance in the Northwest and Its Derivatives*, 38, quoted in Thomas E. Jessett, *Chief Spokane Garry 1811–1892: Christian, Statesman, and Friend of the White Man* (Minneapolis: Denison, 1960) 34.

McLean, who was at Stuart Lake in the northern part of British Columbia during the winter of 1834-36, reported,

> Two young men, natives of Oregon, who had received a little education at Red River, had, on their return to their own country, introduced a sort of religion whose groundwork seemed to be Christianity. This religion spread with amazing rapidity all over the country. It reached Fort Alexandria, the lower post of the district in the autumn of 1834 or 1835.[6]

The spread of Christianity throughout the tribes of the region is further documented by Washington Irving in *The Adventures of Captain Bonneville*:

> During the winter of 1832 Bonneville camped with the Nez Perce on the upper Salmon River. From his experiences he reports of the Nez Perce that "simply to call these people religious would convey but a faint idea of the deep hue of piety and devotion which pervades their whole conduct. Their honesty is immaculate and their purity of purpose...are most remarkable. They are more like a nation of saints than a horde of savages.[7]

The period of 1835 to 1850 saw the first wave of missionaries arrive in Oregon and Washington who came to build missions to teach the Indians Christianity. In 1835 the American Board of Commissioners for Foreign Missions sent Reverend Samuel Parker and his assistant, Marcus Whitman to explore the Columbia River for a possible mission station location. In 1836 Whitman and Henry Spalding and their wives returned to establish the first missions in the Columbia Plateau at Waiilatpu among the Cayuses and at Lapwai among the Nez Perce peoples.[8] The spread of the Word of God during the early 1830s is most noteworthy in that it preceded the arrival of these first missionaries.

With the arrival of the white missionaries, and their "Jamestown brand" of missionary Christianity, the story takes a predictable and unfortunate turn. Just as Puritan missionaries insisted on denouncing Indian ways as demonic more than 200 years earlier, so these white missionaries

---

6. Quoted in Clifford Merrill Drury, *The Diaries and Letters of Henry Harmin Spalding and Asa Bowen Smith Relating to Nez Perce Mission* (Glendale, CA: Clark, 1958) 35.

7. Quoted in Drury, *Diaries and Letters*, 47.

8. Robert Boyd, *Peoples of The Dalles: The Indians of the Wascopam Missions—A Historical Ethnography Based on the Papers of the Free Methodist Missionaries* (Lincoln: University of Nebraska Press 1995) 15.

insisted on European-style Christian worship as well as doctrine. What is worse, their paternalism, ethnocentrism, colonial collusion, and modernism soon "civilized" this movement of the gospel and thus blinded Christians to the prevenient work of God among the Native Americans before the missionaries arrived.

As a direct result of the precedent of Jamestown, an authentic Native American cultural or indigenous expression of following Jesus has never been allowed to develop; the very idea being rejected as syncretistic and incongruous with "biblical" faith. Instead of embracing Jesus as the Creator, the majority of Native Americans blame American Christianity and the church for the loss of their own culture and identity.

## A NATIVE-LED "CONTEXTUALIZATION MOVEMENT"

As I gaze around our Native nations I work hard to resist the temptation to become a complete cynic, harshly critical of Christianity. Despite the history and implications of Jamestown, I nonetheless believe we are in the midst of a historic paradigmatic shift from the paternalism of the past to a genuine Native-led "contextualization movement" of the gospel story.

One way to make some sense of early missionary endeavors is to look at the church through the juxtaposition between Jesus and Christianity, and Christianity and Christendom, the latter being, as professor Peter d'Errico writes in his forward to *Pagans in the Promised Land*, "an alliance of princes and priestly authorities that culminates in the doctrine of divine right of kings and popes."[9] Lamin Sanneh nuances these comparisons a bit differently:

> "World Christianity" is the movement of Christianity as it takes
> form and shape in societies that previously were not Christian,
> societies that had no bureaucratic tradition with which to do-
> mesticate the gospel. In these societies Christianity was received
> and expressed through the cultures, customs, and traditions of the
> people affected. World Christianity is not one thing, but a variety of
> indigenous responses through more or less effective local idioms,
> but in any case without necessarily the European Enlightenment
> frame. "Global Christianity," on the other hand, is the faithful rep-
> lication of Christian forms and patterns developed in Europe. It

9. Peter D'Errico, "Foreword" to Steven T. Newcomb, *Pagans in the Promised Land: Decoding the Doctrine of Christian Discovery* (Golden, CO: Fulcrom, 2008) ix.

echoes Hilaire Belloc's famous statement, "Europe is the faith." It is, in fact, religious establishment and the cultural captivity of faith.[10]

Dr. Tite Tiénou notes that in our day, one should be able to take for granted that Christianity is not the religion of white people. He writes, "Polycentric[11] Christianity is Christian faith with many cultural homes. The fact that Christianity is at home in a multiplicity of cultures, without being permanently wedded to any one of them, presents for Christians everywhere a unique opportunity for examining Christian identity and Christian theology."[12] Yet Phillip Jenkins in *The Next Christendom*, while acknowledging we are undergoing the greatest shift in the history of Christianity, still sees Christianity being inextricably bound up with that of Europe and European-derived civilizations overseas, above all in North America.

> Until recently, the overwhelming majority of Christians have lived in White nations, allowing theorists to speak smugly, arrogantly, of "European Christian" civilization. Conversely, radical writers have seen Christianity as an ideological arm of Western imperialism. Over the past century, however, the center of gravity in the Christian world has shifted inexorably southward, to Africa, Asia, and Latin America.[13]

Thus does Peter D'Errico write, "When we make these important distinctions, we can begin to understand the possibility of differences between the teaching of Jesus and the political and legal doctrines of a church-state complex operating in his name."[14]

While these distinctions help make some sense of things philosophically and ideologically, I remain somewhat bewildered about how to proceed. The fact is that there is a "conglomeration of Euro-American scholars, ministers and lay folk who have, over the centuries, used their

10. Lamin Sanneh, *Whose Religion is Christianity? The Gospel beyond the West* (Grand Rapids: Eerdmans, 2003) 22.

11. Polycentric means having many centers. Rome, America or Western Europe is no longer "the" center of Christian faith, but instead Christianity has many centers or homes.

12. Tite Tiénou, "Indigenous Theologizing: From the Margins to the Center," in *Journal of North America Institute for Indigenous Theological Studies* 3 (2005) 6.

13. Philip Jenkins, *The Next Christendom: The Coming of Global Christianity* (New York: Oxford University Press, 2002) 1, 2.

14. D'Errico, "Foreword" to Newcomb, *Pagans in the Promised Land*, ix.

economic, academic, religious and political dominance to create the illusion that the bible, read through their experience, is the bible read correctly."[15] And it was on the basis of this alleged true reading of the Bible that these men and women, my brothers and sisters, professing faith in Jesus Christ and a commitment to the scriptures, did such oppressive things to Native people, and in many cases, still do. Will they be there waiting to welcome me into heaven when I cross over to the other side? Some days I say, I sure as hell hope not! Someone else maybe, but not me. If God rewards that kind of colonial genocide done in the name of Jesus, with an eternity of blessing, then something is wrong somewhere; could be in me.

With this as a backdrop I will put a little of my tobacco in our common pipe of dialogue for you to smoke on and hopefully enjoy. I hope you find ways to contribute to the "talk story" of this book as you endeavor to live out an honest faith in Jesus in whatever context you live.

## LIMINALITY—CAUGHT IN-BETWEEN

While others have addressed dualism in this volume, let me say that this erroneous dichotomization has been an especially damaging philosophical construct or "religious idealogy" to our Native people. Its influence in the church has created a perceived need for the practice of cultural circumcision as a prerequisite to our Native people becoming or remaining "genuinely" Christian. This is seen most succinctly in the struggle of Native believers to remain connected to notions of identity, which is connected to where they come from, which is the land.

Loss of land, beyond dirt, relates to "sacred space" and its influence in shaping personhood, being and identity; it provides a sense of being from and belonging somewhere. Many First Nations have lost their land completely and their identity or place has diminished along with it. Other Nations have retained their physical lands, but many individuals no longer have a strong connection to their land as a sacred place and their identities with it. A result of prolonged colonization is that our peoples have fallen into a state of liminality wherein transition has become our enduring reality.

---

15. Scot McKnight, *A Community Called Atonement* (Nashville: Abingdon, 2007) 44.

I use liminality as it is used to describe the period in a rite-of-passage ceremony where a child becomes an adult.[16] For a male, at a point, he is no longer a boy, but not yet a man. The ceremony is meant to heighten a sense of being in-between; feelings of confusion, chaos and lostness as he moves from one identity to another. The end result being, a boy now knows he is a man and boyhood activities are now passing/passed away, melting into a new reality/identity of manhood.

As Native people, we are in-between the worlds of yesterday and where we will be; between traditional worldviews and western rationalism; between community and individuality; between spirituality and religion. We are not what we used to be and we are still becoming what we are not yet. In this in-between time we experience confusion, deep loss, fear, the unknown, searching, lostness, despair, our circle is broken. Our identity is constantly stressed, being reshaped, redefined, or altered by the hegemonic assumptions of western Christian dualism, American patriotism or evangelical individualism as we regain our balance in the modern technological world where we live as indigenous peoples.

## THE SECRET ABORIGINAL IDENTITY OF JESUS

Jesus was an aboriginal boy. Jesus was Hebrew. Jesus was born into a traditional Native village. Jesus was a political refugee. Jesus was a cultural man born into the Tribe of Judah. Jesus never doubted his indigenous identity. Jesus overcame colonial oppression. Through his life, death and resurrection, Jesus can heal our broken hoop: "The Word became flesh and blood and moved into the neighbourhood" (John 1:14; Message Version).

Whose "hood" did the Creator of heaven and earth move into? A small Native village named Bethlehem in the land of Palestine in Asia Minor. Jesus was a black-haired, black-eyed and dark complexioned tribal boy—an ethnic boy depending on who gets to call someone else ethnic. He was born a member of the tribal nation of the Hebrew people and sub-tribe of Judah. He was given tribal names; Bright and Morning Star, The Rock, Rose of Sharon, Lion of the Tribe of Judah, Lilly of the Valley, Chief Cornerstone, Daystar and many more.

---

16. A. H. Mathias Zahniser, *Symbol and Ceremony: Making Disciples across Cultures* (Monrovia, CA: MARC 1997), maps a rites of passage process that shows how important this liminality component is to the social, cultural and personal well-being of a person in tribal contexts.

His people, having been invaded and subjugated by a foreign empire, were living under the tyranny of colonial rule. Though His nation was forced to submit to the empirical domination of Rome, Jesus repeatedly spoke of His kingdom as not being of this world. It was not a kingdom of power, oppression and privilege, but love and mutuality. Though Jesus suffered the humiliation of death on the cross at the consent of the colonial magistrate, it did not diminish nor end His kingdom.

After three days in death and hell, he rose from the dead, and in newness of life he set the captives—all human and non-human creation—free from the tyranny of hell and death. He shouts back from the other side saying "Oh grave where is your victory, oh death were is your sting?" As the Waymaker he shows us our way back to the "beauty way." We are redeemed from our brokenness to now love our neighbour, forgive our enemies, care for other broken people and be restored back to authentic community in a broken world.

When Jesus, God-the-Son was baptized in the Jordan River by John the Baptist, as he came out of the water, God-the-Holy-Spirit, like a dove descended on Jesus; then the voice of God-the-Father was heard from heaven saying, "This is my beloved Native boy in whom my heart is deeply pleased." Jesus did not feel ashamed, like a second class citizen, or any sense of inferiority about His dark skin, tribal ways or ethnic identity because he received the affirmation of His Father's and the Holy Spirit's love—in the midst of His tribal identity. God-the-Father was not embarrassed by His Son's obvious ethnic identity.

## *MISSIO DEI*—"MISSION OF GOD"— COMMUNITY IN DIVERSITY

I will dialogue about the "tribalness" of Jesus as a way for us to think about *Missio Dei* as a Trinitarian mutuality model for biblical mission/storytelling. It will serve as a corrective and redemptive lens in addressing the displacement, neocolonial oppression and utter disregard for the value of our First Nations/indigenous people. One of the obvious implications of Jamestown is that today, we remain absent from the church as co-equal participants in the life, work and gospel telling of Jesus Christ among the Nations; we only exist in the American church as it's perpetual mission field; needy recipients, unreached peoples, marginalized, etc. Redemptively, at the core of *missio Dei* is the discovery of "place" for indigenous people.

Phillip Potter sees *Missio Dei* presenting a radical departure from a western ecclesiocentric focus to a Trinitarian focus.[17] In light of the astonishing kingdom possibilities this view of mission/story-telling represents, especially for our First Nations/indigenous people, I find its conspicuous absence from church pulpits and popular Christian writing to be ludicrous and distressing.

*Missio Dei* can be thought of in terms of the extension of God's "village" life in the story of the coming of Jesus and the abiding presence of the Holy Spirit in Creation; it is Creator's invitation to be restored in relationship within the village of God.

> Trinitarian theology points to the radical communal nature of God. This communion overflows into an involvement with history that aims at drawing humanity and creation in general into this communion with God's very life. God's very nature, therefore, is missionary. It is not primarily about the propagation or transmission of intellectual convictions, doctrines, moral commands, etc., but rather about the inclusion of all creation in God's overflowing, superabundant life of communion. The church's missionary nature derives from its participation in this overflowing Trinitarian life.[18]

I find in the *Missio Dei* a place of identity, belonging, value, peace, justice and affirmation—*Shalom*—for Indigenous people. That place, however, does not, and has not existed in missionary efforts among our tribal people. The Bible expresses the same reality of the new humanity in the word *shalom*. Potter would say the goal towards which God is working, the ultimate end of his mission, is the establishment of *shalom*, which intrinsically involves the realization of the full potentialities of ALL creation—human and non-human—and its ultimate reconciliation and unity in Christ.[19]

The "outcomes" of a Trinitarian centered focus of the *Missio Dei* described by Bevans and Schroeder are "building vibrant community life, where real sharing, mutuality, service and solidarity take place."[20] In this place people experience genuine local autonomy and cultural exis-

17. Philip Potter, *Life in All its Fullness* (Geneva: World Council of Churches, 1981).

18. Stephen Bevans and Roger Schroeder, *Constants in Context: A Theology of Mission for Today* (Maryknoll, NY: Orbis, 1994) 288–89.

19. Potter, *Life in All its Fullness*, 104.

20. Bevans and Schroeder, *Constants in Context*, 298.

tence that thrives, as well as a real sense of communion with other local churches and Christians of other cultural groups. This picture of a Trinitarian based *Missio Dei* has the feel of village life. As the dominance of western, modernist worldview assumptions decline in light of the shift of Christianity from the north to the south and west to east, *Missio Dei* has huge implications for the future of mission/story-telling as an expression of community.

## *MISSIO DEI* AS A NEW PARADIGM: A TRINITARIAN BASED THEOLOGY OF MISSION/STORY-TELLING

Bevans and Schroeder identify the mutual openness of Father and Son, Son and Spirit, Spirit and Father as a model of relationship, "the constitutive nature of relationship for personal identity, the inclusion of diversity in community—all these vital truths and practices are rooted in Trinitarian reality and existence."[21]

The Holy Spirit presided over the earth/creation while it lay void, waste and dark. As he hovered, like a chicken over its yet unhatched eggs, the life of God began to touch all of the earth at a cosmic and molecular level, dispelling the darkness, bringing divine order and filling the earth with the life of God. The earth was now "nine-months pregnant" with plants, animals and even human beings. When God wanted to create plants he delivered them out of the belly of the earth.

> Then God said, "Let the earth sprout vegetation, plants yielding seed, and fruit trees on the earth bearing fruit after their kind with seed in them"; and it was so. The earth brought forth vegetation, plants yielding seed after their kind, and trees bearing fruit with seed in them, after their kind; and God saw that it was good. (Gen 1:11,12)

When he wanted to create animals, he delivered them out of the belly of the earth.

> Then God said, "Let the earth bring forth living creatures after their kind: cattle and creeping things and beasts of the earth after their kind"; and it was so. God made the beasts of the earth after their kind, and the cattle after their kind, and everything that creeps on the ground after its kind; and God saw that it was good. (Gen 1:24, 25)

21. Bevans and Schroeder, *Constants in Context*, 288.

When it came time to create human beings, he created Male-Man and Female-Man in his likeness and image and delivered them out of the dust of the earth.

> Then God said, "Let Us make man in Our image, according to Our likeness; and let them rule over the fish of the sea and over the birds of the sky and over the cattle and over all the earth, and over every creeping thing that creeps on the earth." God created man in His own image, in the image of God He created him; male and female He created them. (Gen 1:26, 27)

> Then the LORD God formed man of dust from the ground, and breathed into his nostrils the breath of life; and man became a living being. (Gen 2:7)

The *Missio Dei* as Trinitarian faith calls us to "recognize the interconnectedness of everything in the universe. Everything is related to everything else, and this means that an anthropology in the light of the Trinity can never be one that is anthropocentric." Since everything is connected, humanity is part of the whole of creation[22] and the whole of creation is part of our human identity. And everything that "never was," has ever been, or ever shall be, came first, "existed," within the community of the Father, Son and Holy Spirit before it proceeded out from them.

## WE ARE ALL RELATIVES IN THE *MISSIO DEI*

In Genesis, the human/creation story emerges from within the radical community of the Trinity and the oneness within the diversity of the Father, Son and Holy Spirit. In Revelation, it "ends" with the radical community of the Trinity and the oneness within the diversity of the Father, Son and Holy Spirit, with human beings fully participating, have been restored to *imago Dei*. "After these things I looked, and behold, a great multitude which no one could number, of all nations, tribes, peoples, and tongues, standing before the throne and before the Lamb" (Rev. 7:9).

On the basis of both the Genesis and Revelation accounts no people or race should regard itself as superior or inferior in origin or essence. What John saw in Revelation was birthed out of God's self. The diversity in heaven is the reality of what God intended to be from the very beginning because only in the diversity of humanity could the indescribableness of God be "mirrored." With these as bookends, the *Missio Dei* is a home

22. Bevans and Schroeder, *Constants in Context*, 301.

for indigenous people in the story of Creation. Arthur Glasser sees it as striking that the Old Testament regards human beings as constituting one great family: "The unity of the human race is an unassailable reality."[23]

Ontologically *Missio Dei* is like the North Star for a sailor. It provides us a constant point of reference from which we reorient ourselves as to who we are and where we come from and where we are currently situated.

In the *Missio Dei*, as "observable" in Revelation, heavenly worship reflects in its perfected state that which from the beginning of time always existed in the Trinity; here we see diversity perfected, cultures flourish, creation restored and the radical self-giving oneness of the community of the redeemed—the divine *tiyospaye*—"extended family"[24] worshipping the Creator. Cultural diversity is not a deviation from God's "original plan," the result of sin or judgment at Babel, but has always been God's intention and design for human beings. This is good news for Indigenous people and affirms our "place" as Native/indigenous people within the context of God's eternal triune community and purposes for creation

Among the Lakota/Sioux, *Mitakuye Oyasin* is an expression that captures this heavenly reality. Translated, the words say, "All My Relatives or Relations." However, what is communicated is a sense of one's connectedness to the bigger world of creation. It says I am part of the people who have gone before me, with the people living today, and with those who will come after me. It says I am related to things above, things below and things all around. It says I am a small part of all that is, and ever has been, sacred. It militates against the sacred/secular dichotomy of the West and aligns us with a holistic and integrated worldview orientation of the *Missio Dei.*

*Missio Dei* has a reconciliation dynamic that calls us to love others. Jesus says to love our enemies and to pray for those who deceitfully use us. *Mitakuye Oyasin*, according to Native (Osage) theologian George Tinker, includes as our relatives, not only those of our immediate family but also "fellow tribal members or even all Indian people."[25] Going even further, the *Missio Dei* reminds us of "first things" and compels us to love

23. Arthur F. Glasser, *Announcing the Kingdom: The Story of God's Mission in the Bible* (Grand Rapids: Baker, 2003) 36.

24. *Tiyospaye* ("tee-yo'shpa-yea") a Lakota/Sioux word that means extended family.

25. George E. Tinker, *Spirit and Resistance: Political Theology and American Indian Liberation* (Minneapolis: Fortress, 2003) 92.

all "two-leggeds"; even those who have hurt, wounded, unjustly treated, killed, and oppressed our people.

# 6

# Salvation History and the Mission of God

## Implications for the Mission of the Church among Native Americans

RICHARD E. WALDROP AND J. L. CORKY ALEXANDER JR.

*Since all mission originates and proceeds from God, the divine missionary nature is revealed through God's great salvific acts in history which are mediated by the great missionary Spirit. This is revealed biblically in creation, in the covenant and formation of Israel, the incarnation of God in the person of Jesus of Nazareth. It continues in the world through the church from Pentecost toward the consummation of all things in Christ Jesus in the eschaton. The Church fulfills her holistic mission as she is faithful to the missionary character of God. The church's mission to and among Native Americans, therefore, must be judged historically by its faithfulness, or lack thereof, to the revealed missionary character of God and by its cultural appropriateness through redemptive analogical mission methods.*

## THE CHRISTIAN MISSION AND NATIVE AMERICA

All mission begins in and emanates from the Triune God. In this way the missionary character of God is revealed. Our God is a missionary God and so the life of the Church must be characterized as missionary existence.[1] Christian faith is intrinsically missionary, or as the Swiss theologian, Emil Brunner, has said, "the Church exists by mission, just as fire

---

1. David Bosch, *Transforming Mission: Paradigm Shifts in Theology of Mission* (Maryknoll, NY: Orbis, 1992) 9.

exists by burning."[2] Having made those foundational statements, additional questions always arise concerning the particularities of Christian mission. The "why" and the "how" of mission, as an ecclesial and human enterprise, rest upon the missionary character of the Triune God.

Concerning Christian mission among indigenous peoples of the Americas, there are several vital issues that must be taken into account when developing a mission theology. First, the variegated history of violence, subjugation, and oppression perpetrated upon Native cultures in the name of Christ is well documented (de las Casas, Dussell, Galeano, Lernox, Brown, Deloria, and Josephy come to mind). From the Patagonian steppes of southern Argentina to the arctic regions of the north, this land of Abya Yala or Turtle Island and its peoples have been stained with the blood of destruction and pillage suffered at the hands of so-called missionaries and mission agencies of all varieties—first the Roman Catholics, then Protestants, Fundamentalist Evangelicals, and most recently even Neo-Pentecostals. As a concrete example of the latter, we were appalled by the atrocities, in the 1980s, of the so-called born-again dictator, General Efrain Rios Montt, a member and elder of the Verbo Church, and his army's practice of military genocide against the Mayan indigenous peoples of Guatemala. While there have been notable exceptions to the above sweeping acusations, our efforts at true repentance, not to mention making restitution where possible, have been, unfortunately, too little and too late. And for all who believe all of this to be in the distant past, it is necessary to denounce the "impure motives" of colonial and neo-colonial imperialism, cultural superiority, and ecclesiastical territorialism practiced during the "modern missionary era" by Western mission agencies and missionaries.[3] Further, those of us who seek to do mission with and among indigenous peoples must distance ourselves from the cultural captivity of the un-civil "civil religion" and the Constantinianism of the imperial church of North America.

But second, we must allow the biblical witness to speak prophetically and challenge us in regards to the peaceable and wholistic nature of Christian mission. In regards to Native Americans, Dr. Randy Woodley

---

2. Emil Brunner, *The Word and the World* (London: SCM, 1931) 108; cf. Bosch, *Transforming Mission*, 8.

3. Bosch, *Transforming Mission*, "Introduction."

(Keetoowah Cherokee),[4] contrasts two very different mission spiritualities that can be adopted from scripture:

> One is reflected through what might be termed a *"shalom* spirituality"* marked by welcoming strangers, keeping Sabbath years, becoming a light to the nations, etc. Another model develops in Israel as a kind of "nation-state spirituality," marked by conquest, ethnocentrism and hegemony. In the latter paradigm, *shalom* is co-opted and horded which perverted it into an evil theology that promotes an evil spirituality.[5]

We must return, not only to biblical theology, but to the center of Scripture and Christian mission, the Gospel, and to the center of the Gospel, which is Jesus and his central teaching concerning the Reign of God, whose basic spiritual and ethical principles are found in the Sermon on the Mount. The earliest Christian communities and the later Anabaptist traditions have much to teach us in this regard. Many early Pentecostal leaders and denominations also had clear pacifist statements concerning the role of Christians, the deadly use of violence, and participation in war and military enterprises. This Gospel of peace must find a way of tapping into the various peace traditions of the indigenous peoples of this hemisphere, even as it challenges the tendencies of violence also found there. Woodley helps us to understand that such Native tribes as the Cheyenne have their own peace tradition contrary to stereotypes.

> Even among those tribes who have gained a reputation as "warlike" in the American experience, there existed striking counterbalances in their structure and philosophy to war. One such example is that of the Cheyenne "Peace Chiefs." According to the teachings of Sweet Medicine, the most revered Cheyenne Teacher and Prophet, all forty-four chiefs among them must be Peace Chiefs. Even to-

---

4. Dr. Randy Woodley (Keetoowah Cherokee) founded and directs Eagles Wings Ministry in Newburg, Oregon. He is a leader in the Native North American Contextual Movement. His writings include *Living in Color: Embracing God's Passion for Ethnic Diversity* (Downers Grove, IL: InterVarsity) 2001; *Mixed Blood, Not Mixed Up: Finding God-Given Identity in a Multi-Cultural World* (Wilmore, KY: By the author, 2004); and *When Going to Church Is Sin and Other Essays on Native American Christian Missions* (Scotland, PA: Healing the Land, 2007).

5. Randy Woodley, "The Native American Harmony Ethic (in Relation to the Trinity and Shalom) as a Foundation for Mission" (unpublished paper, 2005) 5.

day, Sweet Medicine's words are repeated at the inauguration of every new chief.[6]

As we begin to chart a biblical mission theology then, our efforts at evangelization among indigenous peoples must be culturally relevant, contextual, and Spirit-directed. The Great Missionary Spirit of God has been present among Native peoples in this part of the world long before any of our European ancestors arrived here. Following the lead of the Spirit, then, we must find ways to affirm and appreciate the beauty of the arts and traditions, the integrity of the worldviews, and the value of material culture in the defense of the interests of both Native American peoples and of the Gospel we seek to proclaim and live. One way of ministering in Native contexts is to use "redemptive analogies" found in the culture and to correlate these with the Gospel.[7] This brings what Rev. Kyle Taylor (Pawnee/Choctaw) calls "common ground" ministry,[8] which many Native Americans have embraced.

Our ultimate aim is to see the *shalom*, or salvation, of God come to fruition in individual lives healed, and in families, communities and tribes restored by the power of the Gospel. Woodley believes

> there is room in the "Native American Old Testament" for a similar theological construct, one that especially can provide a basis for Native American views of harmony, in a similar way that *shalom* was developed in Judaism. Similar to Choctaw theologian Steve Charleston, who may have coined the phrase, "Native American Old Testament," "[t]oday I feel comfortable talking about a Christianity that emerges from Native America." When considering the link between *shalom* in Judaism and the nature of the Trinity, it is easy to see why *shalom* is perhaps the ideal one word that we can use to both describe God and to understand God's vision for all humanity. Although there is only sparse evidence that some Native American tribes held a trinitarian view of God, our indigenous harmony ethic, which I will describe later, is, in many ways, synonymous with biblical *shalom*. Therefore, an informed Native American theology of the Trinity can provide further in-

---

6. Woodley, "Native American Harmony Ethic," 27.

7. Which has also been popularized by missionary Don Richardson, *Eternity in Their Hearts* (Ventura, CA: Regal, 1984).

8. Kyle Taylor, interview by Corky Alexander, Muskogee, Oklahoma, 17 February 2009.

sight into God, and also serve as a solid basis of mission for Native Americans to the rest of the world.[9]

To those ends we now turn our attention more directly to the biblical narrative.

## THE MISSIONARY GOD IN CREATION

In creation, God is revealed as "Missionary," if by missionary we understand the idea that God is "Self-sent," "Self-extended," and "Self-revealed" outwardly through the divine creational activity. In Genesis, we find one of the great principles of missionary existence: the creative desire and ability to open oneself outwardly and take concrete steps to draw near to others with the intention of entering into relationships which seek the welfare and salvation of others.

In fact, the original foundation of this principle rests upon the social and communal nature of "trinitarian mutuality,"[10] or the Economic Trinity. In the first words registered in Sacred Scripture, it is revealed to us that it was the Spirit (breath or wind) of God which moved upon the empty and void "face of the deep" as the Creator Spirit (feminine voice) of Life. In the history of Christian thought, the Spirit of God has been recognized in her missionary role as the agent which generates and sustains life in all its dimensions.[11] Consequentially, to believe in the Triune God and to do mission in trinitarian fashion is an affirmation of full and abundant life, and must be, at the same time, a negation of anything which diminishes or destroys the life of the creation including, especially, human life in its spiritual, social and physical sense.

In regards to the various missionary ventures of the Church (missions or *missiones ecclesiae*),[12] it should also be recognized that the Spirit precedes and inspires all legitimate ecclesial and human initiatives, as an already active missionary presence in the world. Woodley states:

---

9. Woodley, "Native American Harmony Ethic," 3. The Charleston reference in the quotation can be found in *Native and Christian: Indigenous Voices on Religious Identity in the United States and Canada*, ed. James Treat (New York: Routledge, 1996) 69.

10. Jürgen Moltmann, *The Spirit of Life: A Universal Affirmation*, trans. Margaret Kohl (Minneapolis: Fortress, 1992) 71–72 and 248–66.

11. Moltmann, *Spirit of Life*, 144–60.

12. Bosch, *Transforming Mission*, 10.

> Our ancient Indian people on Turtle Island (North America) knew God. Many tribes have their own stories of covenant with the Creator. Each tribe had stories of land areas given to them by the Creator. In the most real sense of the word, "relationship" was made between the Great Spirit and the people of this continent and this relationship between God, the people and the land is the source for development of their spirituality. These North American tribal covenant stories, songs, ceremonies, societies, prophets, etc. are what we can correctly call each tribe's "Old Testament" experience.[13]

In this way, we understand that from the beginning, we follow and participate in the missionary initiative of the Triune God and not our own. This must be re-affirmed with firmness and clarity, especially in a time in which Christian mission has been twisted and confused, too often, with impure motives and equivocal actions related to neo-liberal economic imperialism, attitudes of cultural and spiritual superiority, the manipulation of resources by the cultures of consumerism and "prosperity," and the corresponding *un*civil "civil religion" in the Global North at the expense of the majority cultures and Pentecostal churches of the Global South.

Regarding the missionary nature of the social Trinity, the words registered in Genesis 1:26 are illustrative: "*let us* make humankind in *our* image, according to *our* likeness." The *Missio Dei* is an enterprise which is realized in divine community. The mission of the Church, under the *Missio Dei,* must be carried out among all the sectors and groups which comprise the ecclesial community, and not simply by a group of "professional missionaries" who too often form an elite class of "super-spiritual" individuals.

The biblical idea of the image of God, or *imago Dei,* in human beings, also has clear missiological implications. Human beings, because they carry the image of God and because they are the creation of God, must be treated with dignity and justice. Therefore, the whole missionary enterprise of the Church has as one of its principal objectives the recognition of the value of human life in all of its dimensions. In the case of mission among Native Americans, this includes the dignification, appreciation and appropriation of the many artistic cultural expressions which grow out of worldviews which are strongly connected to the experience of the immanance of God's Spirit and other supernatural phenomena.

---

13. Woodley, "Native American Harmony Ethic," 4.

Because God is the Spirit of Life, the Church must be clear in her prophetic proclamation of the dignity of life and in her prophetic denunciation of violence, slavery, racism, abortion, addiction, poverty, and war, which are all instruments of sin, death and destruction.[14] This is a truly a completely "whole life" position. Holistic Christian mission signifies the full humanization and dignification of life in light of the image of God in each human being.

In addition to what is said above, in the creation story registered in Genesis, it is clear that the mission of God is delegated and shared, in the first instance, with human beings, that is to say, with the first human couple, Adam and Eve. In this way, the mission becomes a commission. This fact also points clearly to the social nature of the Trinity. God's first discourse directed to human beings in Genesis 1:28–30, has been referred to as the *cultural mandate*.[15] Here are also references to human participation regarding the stewardship or care of the natural environment or God's creation. From this point we see emerging the idea of an ecological responsibility which should occupy an important space in the missiological agenda of the Church. In addition to the environmental responsibility given to human beings, the symbiotic human-ecological relationship is established with the result of providing wellbeing and sustainability to the inhabitants of the planet. For Native Americans, it is more than a stewardship. The Gospel previously presented to Native peoples has not appreciated the particular role of land. Woodley helps us again.

> What has not been presented clearly to Native Americans is the following storyline: Jesus, as the Creator-Son, brought the good news of the relational aspects of the trinitarian God to earth by creating a *place*. Eden was where human beings were first placed to enjoy the fullest possible sense of *place* on earth. God's original intention was to allow humans to relate in the parameters of the garden, a *shalom* garden. One could say that the garden culture was the original human culture from which one could come to know God, a God who relates in and through community. This divine community is a model for all human societies including

14. On the issue of war and peace from a Pentecostal perspective, see the many pacifist statements issued by early Pentecostal leaders and denominations through the twentieth century, compiled at the Thirdway Peace and Justice Fellowship-San Fransisco website (www.thirdway.cc.)

15. Pablo Deiros, *Diccionario hispanoamericano de la misión* (Miami: COMIBAM, 1997) 267.

Native Americans. It is this story to which Native Americans can relate, because it is the same story we already know in our own context and in our own *place*.[16]

This relationship between God, creation and human beings is established within the framework of social responsibility and submission to divine purpose.[17] With the human disobedience and sin registered in Genesis 3, the panorama of human life, and as a result, creation, is altered dramatically, although not irreversibly. For this reason, the *Missio Dei* and the *Missio ecclesiae* are directed toward the restoration of full life which would later reach its zenith in the redemption effectuated by the Son of God, Jesus of Nazareth, on the cross which is situated at center stage of salvific history. The good news of the incarnation of God in human history and of a new way of living (the Reign of God) would become the heart of evangelization and would occupy the center of the missionary task of the Church.

In this sense, the whole plan of God's mission revealed in the Old Testament should be seen in anticipation of its definitive fulfillment in the death and resurrection of Jesus Christ, finding its course in a commission or mandate given by him to his followers who would form the Church empowered for mission by the Holy Spirit. In this way, the Church participates in the *Missio Dei* as sign, agent and sacrament unto the consummation of the Reign of God at the *eschaton*.

## INCARNATIONAL MISSION

In creation, the missionary God is self-revealed, and self-sent toward that which did not yet exist. This was a gesture of supreme creativity in a desire to extend divine relational capacity outwardly. Now in the specifically human context, the incarnation constitutes God's second great act of universal scope and cosmic redemption.

The attempt at explicating the fact that God "bore" a Son and that this Father God "sent" his Son into the world certainly transcends the capacity of human reason and must remain, to a great degree, a mystery of divine

---

16. Woodley, "Native American Harmony Ethic," 11.

17. See, for example, the excellent work done recently by an interdisciplinary and interdenominational task force which issued "An Urgent Call to Action: Scientists and Evangelicals Unite to Protect Creation," in *National Press Club* (Washington, DC, January 17, 2007).

grace. But even as it is a mystery, the incarnation reveals to us much of the nature of the *Missio Dei*. The noble missionary ideal of opening oneself and of risking one's own existence for the good of someone or something else, has its origin in the salvific history of a humanized and crucified God.[18] The incarnation, then, establishes the pattern for all subsequent missionary activity in various ways. It is not only opening oneself, but also is the fact of *being sent on mission* for the purpose of the salvation of others. Etymologically, the word "mission" carries with it the indispensable element of the action of sending.[19] It also signifies becoming like the other or identifying oneself with the condition of the other persons to whom one is sent. This idea is well expressed in the words of a popular Latin American gospel chorus,

> I am sent by God
> and my hand is ready
> to build a fraternal world with Him,
> The angels have not been sent to change
> a world of pain into a world of peace,
> It has fallen to me to make this a reality,
> Help me, Lord, to do your will.[20]

From the earliest times of Christianity, then, mission has carried the trinitarian idea of divine sending:[21] the Father is self-sent *in* creation, and later sent *to* creation in the incarnation of the Son, Jesus Christ, and at the same time the Holy Spirit is sent *to and throughout* the world as the divine agent of the *Missio Dei*.

Jesus of Nazareth, sent from God, is the missionary *par excellence*, and is the perfect model of what holistic and liberating mission means.[22] In the inauguration of his ministry and announcement of his messianic platform in the synagogue of Nazareth, Jesus textually cites the prophetic passage of Isaiah 61, making it his own. He proclaims himself as

18. Jürgen Moltmann, *The Crucified God: The Cross of Christ as the Foundation and Cristicism of Christian Theology*, trans. Margaret Kohl (New York: Harper & Row, 1974) 4.

19. Horst Rzepkowski, *Diccionario de misionologia: Historia, teologia, etnologia* (Navarra, Spain: Editorial Verbo Divino, 1997) 357–58.

20. Author unknown, but originating in Cuba according to Dr. Reinerio Arce, Rector of the Seminario Evangelico Unido de Mantanzas, Cuba.

21. Bosch, *Transforming Mission*, 1–2.

22. Dario López Rodriguez, *La mision liberadora de Jesus: El mensaje del evangelio de Lucas,* (Lima, Peru: Puma Ediciones, 2004) 46.

the Sent One from God and Anointed of the Spirit to preach good news to the poor.

In terms of the context of his birth, Jesus of Nazareth is indeed the "aboriginal boy" and lives as an eternal guide to understanding the realities of Native people in their tribal experience.[23] This "tribalness" of Jesus introduces to the true meaning of *Missio Dei*, and bears hope for rescue from the white superiority that so dominates traditional North American missions.

From the specific particularity of the geographical and social location of Galilee, and from the point of departure of Jesus' identification with the repugnant lepers, abused women, forgotten children and marginalized Samaritans, Jesus demonstrates the way of mission. It is the road of solidarity with those who suffer persecution, the poor in spirit, those who are thirsty for righteousness, the humble peacemakers, those who are merciful and of a pure heart: because the Reign of God belongs to them (Matthew 5:3–12).

However, one cannot speak adequately of the incarnational mission of the Triune God without recognizing the medullar place of the *cross*. The cross is situated at center stage of salvific history and constitutes the hinge upon which the *kairós* of God turns. Everything before it anticipates it, and all that proceeds from it depends upon it as it is remembered. God's entire salvific work is sealed upon the cross and there "it is completed" (John 19:30). In regard to mission, then, the cross is the example and the reminder of the suffering and martyrdom which is required of all faithful missionaries. On the road of mission there will be sacrifice, cross, and death, for the sake of reaching others with salvation. But, after the cross of death comes the victory of the resurrection, and after the sacrifice and martyrdom of mission comes the full life of redemption in persons who are evangelized, in societies that are transformed, and in the creation that is renewed.

Unfortunately, however, the genocide perpetuated by white colonial missionaries upon Native peoples has left a darkness upon the history of North American missions and surely upon the hearts of participating denominational missionaries. To see the reconciliation and restitution which is consistent with the gospel message come to reality in our land, it is necessary for the Church to accompany and respond to the Indians' quest

23. See Richard Twiss' chapter in this volume; cf. Twiss, *One Church Many Tribes: Following Jesus the Way God Made You* (Ventura, CA: Regal, 2000).

for reparation. The sinful failure of Euro-American missionaries to follow in the Spirit of the cross will forever shadow any attempts to embody transformational messengers.[24]

The evangelical message of the life, death and resurrection of Jesus Christ was and always shall be: "The time has been fulfilled and the Reign of God has come near; repent and believe on the Gospel" (Mark 1:15). The Reign of God, then, becomes the vertebral cord of Christian mission and seeks the restoration of "all things" in Christ Jesus (Revelation 21:5). The Church, as such, is not the final goal of the *Missio Dei*, but the penultimate goal.[25] The Church belongs to the Reign of God, but God's Reign extends beyond the Church. The Reign of God is the realization of the final goal of the full manifestation of God's *shalom* in the world, when in the *parusía* of Jesus Christ all that has been created will be completely renewed and the image of God will be totally recuperated in all of humanity at the eschaton.

## PENTECOSTAL MISSION

In the interim, we continue to move forward in the missionary age of the missionary Church by the power of the missionary Spirit.[26] The Church has been chosen as an indispensable instrument in the "hands" of God in the fulfillment of the divine mission. The Church may not be the only instrument available to divine agency but has been called out (*ecclesia*) to occupy a singular place of special prominence and privilege in the vanguard of God's mission. As John the Baptist prophetically made the way straight in preparation for the coming of the Son of God (Matthew 3:1–17), in the same way, the true Church prepares the way for the coming and final consummation of the Reign of God.

The faithful Church continually lives the experience of the "coming and going" of mission. She is called to union with God in Jesus Christ, to the communion (fellowship) of the saints, and to reunion (meeting) for temporal worship. But she is also called to go out in the dispersion of mission, in evangelization and in the transformation of life in all its facets.

24. See William R. Burrows's chapter in this volume.

25. Orlando Costas, "Crecimiento integral y palabra de Dios," in *Iglesia y Mision* 2:1 (1983) 6. Also, see Costas, *The Integrity of Mission: The Inner Life and Outreach of the Church* (New York: Harper & Row, 1979) 56–57.

26. Jürgen Moltmann, *The Church in the Power of the Spirit: A Contribution to Messianic Ecclesiology*, trans. Margaret Kohl (Minneapolis: Fortress, 1993) 7–11.

In this sense, the mission of the Church has a *centrifugal* character somewhat distinct from the *centripetal* character of that of the Old Testament people of God.[27] Said differently, the Church moves from the center of her faith, worship, and commitment to Christ toward the periphery of mission in the world and, in this way, overcomes the multiple barriers of time and space, culture and race, and idiom and ideology.

The Holy Spirit is always the agent of mission, the Great Spirit who goes before and reveals the Creator through cultural rituals, preceding the force and power of the Gospel.[28] The Spirit animates the church-in-mission so that, in the words of the Lausanne Covenant affirmed at the International Congress on World Evangelization in Lausanne, Switzerland in 1974, "the whole Church will take the whole Gospel to the whole world."[29] Under this rubric, the Jewish Festival of Pentecost (Acts 2) becomes not only a celebration of another annual cycle of Spring harvest, but the beginning of a new, end-times, worldwide cycle of ingathering by the Lord of the harvest (Matthew 9:38), with the sending out of workers so that the mission of God will be carried out in the world. Pentecost has the significance of both missionary event and movement. It is the humble and insignificant Galilean peasants who are converted into the protagonists and actors at the center stage of divine mission as they lend their voices to the xenolalia of the Spirit so that the festive representatives of the "united nations" in Jerusalem are able to capture the salvific significance of the death, resurrection, and ascension of Jesus and thereby answer the question which spontaneously arose from the multitude, "What is the meaning of this?" (Acts 2:12).

Pentecost, then, represents a new wind of the Spirit with the same character of the breath of creation life imparted by the Spirit of God as she brooded over the face of the deep on the first day of creation, and

---

27. Deiros, *Diccionario*, 287.

28. There is in an affinity between Native Americans and Jewish people, in that they share the experience of having been a tribal people who the Creator revealed Himself through their traditions before the Christian gospel came to be preached to them. Rev. Kyle Taylor (Pawnee/Choctaw) has pointed out one ancient Pawnee name for Creator which designates Him as "one who walks on water." This bears the question, "How did they know He walks on water, if He did not appear to them?" Kyle Taylor, interview by Corky Alexander, Muskogee, Oklahoma, 17 February 2009.

29. See Article No. 6 of the Lausanne Covenant in Gerald H. Anderson and Thomas F. Stransky, CSP, eds., *Mission Trends No. 2: Evangelization* (New York: Paulist, 1975) 239–48.

gave life to the first human beings on the sixth day of creation (Genesis 1:1, 27–31). Pentecost also signifies the purifying, sanctifying fire of God, which cleanses and separates the people from the profane unto the sacred uses of missionary service, such as what happened to the people of God when the fire fell on Mount Sinai (Exodus 19). Pentecost is the prophetic and miraculous announcement of the good news of the Reign of God in Christ Jesus in the languages of the world, represented that day by the various delegations of pilgrims gathered in Jerusalem.

As a result of Pentecost, the people of God, the Church, is revived by the Spirit for her mission in the world and through her existence begins to demonstrate the evangelical values of communion one with another, of the sharing of bread and other belongings (including properties), and of perseverance in the teachings of Jesus Christ and the apostles (Acts 2:42–47; Matthew 28:18–20).

Finally, in the new post-Pentecost era, eschatological hope comes to play a catalytic role which orients, motivates, and mobilizes the mission of the Church in its multiple expressions (word, sign, deed), dimensions (incarnational, liturgical, diaconal, numerical), and directions (vertical, horizontal).[30] Far from giving in to an escapist scheme of a rigid fundamentalist eschatology, or of falling prey to a neo-liberal economic, globalizing ideology, or imperialistic neo-colonial politics—all too often practiced by Western missionaries among Native Americans—Christian mission recovers new energies in the promise of God to liberate the whole creation so that on the final day of the eschaton, the Day of the Lord, the great multitude from all the nations, tribes, people, and tongues, will cry in a loud voice saying, "Salvation belongs to our God who is seated on the throne, and to the Lamb" (Rev 7:9–10). Then, the *missio dei trinitaria*, will be completed, having finished its course from the Creation, to the Covenant, to the Incarnation and the Cross, and passing through Pentecost until the Consummation of all things in Christ Jesus to the glory of the Triune God!

---

30. Jürgen Moltmann, *Theology of Hope: On the Ground and the Implictions of a Christian Eschatology* (Minneapolis: Fortress, 1993) 353–76; Steven Land, *Pentecostal Spirituality: A Passion of the Kingdom* (Sheffield, England: Sheffield, 1993) 122–81; and Juan B. Stam, *Profecía bíblica y misión de la Iglesia* (Quito, Ecuador: Consejo Latinoamericano de Iglesias, 2004) 98–102.

## IMPLICATIONS FOR NATIVE AMERICAN MISSIONS

This dialogue between hearts must transform the actual carrying out of the *Missio Dei*. Non-Native leaders continue to dominate denominational efforts, which repeatedly perpetuate a tainted and painful model, a poor representation of what Christ died to bring. In line with the principle of incarnational and pentecostal mission explicated above, several changes are demanded.

First, Native or indigenous leadership, which holds great promise,[31] must be instituted in demoninational and organizational contexts. The fear that there are not enough trained Natives should be eased with the realization of the existence of the sophisticated scholarship evidenced in such venues as the North American Institute for Indigenous Theological Studies. Native ministries may need to be inter-tribal in places. The Foursquare Church has a testimony of success in appointing Native leaders over their own districts, which are inter-tribal. This has already happened in some places for years, but the continued presence of white leaders directing Native missions is embarrassing.[32]

As Native and non-Native leaders join together as co-equals in ministry, there may need to be a type of Truth and Reconciliation Commision approach to seek healing from the past.[33] This will not happen until indigenous leadership is in place. Fear and prejudice toward contextual efforts must be removed through open minded prayerful reflection as Native leaders are encouraged to discern their own communities and practices. It is time for whites to stop acting patronizingly on behalf of Native people. The denominational and organizational attempts in Native American missions must move from benevolence-based approaches to one that empowers the types of community development that only indigenous leadership can provide. Indigenous leadership must then take the lead to ensure that Native American worldviews and whatever results or

---

31. Institute, American Indian Research and Policy, "Traditional American Indian Leadership: A Comparison with U.S. Governance," available at http://www.airpi.org/research/tradlead.html. Native leadership characteristics are more Christian in that they are communal and consensual over and against political and hierchical.

32. This is especially embarrassing in the light of the fact that Roland Allen made a broad call for this in 1962, and missiologists have been well acquainted with it. See Roland Allen, *The Spontaneous Expansion of the Church and the Causes Which Hinder It* (1962; reprint, Grand Rapids: Eerdmans, 1971).

33. See Desmond Tutu, *No Future without Forgiveness* (New York: Doubleday, 1999).

recommendations of any reconciliation efforts are widely shared through publications and Native ministerial training must be empowered, that is both by and for Native peoples. Then as mission projects unfold under indigenous direction, denominational resources must be continued as the non-Native leaders join together with the Native American communities to seek reparation for the losses they deserve.

Native Americans and other indigenous peoples have been raised up to lead us in not only reaching the world and its tribes, but to both the healing of internal scars such as post traumatic stress syndrome and the re-balancing of cosmic forces overturned by human actions. Many Native ceremonies have served effectively as preparation for and healing/cleansing from wartime woundedness and other social ills. In a few places, Natives are contextualizing these as Christian healing services. These kinds of rites may also, by extension, ultimately hold the keys to the preservation of the earth itself, which a lack of appreciation and adherence to a Native perspective has left in danger of devastation.

To focus on one example, Native Americans are sorely underserved in terms of governmental funding for the developmentally disabled despite the fact that twenty-two percent of their population is developmentally disabled due to fetal alcohol syndrome. This issue is a national emergency that cannot wait for the government to act alone. The Church must act promptly by acting in favor of legislation that provides funding for the only minority not covered under Title VI. Natives must direct these efforts due to the time/space differences in worldview,[34] as well as the differences in ideas related to what it means to be well. Non-Natives tend to fall into the typical medical approaches that serve a non-Native worldview. There are other approaches that do not include rigid appointments and respect the age old Native uses of minerals and plants, which predated the Euro-American pharmacy. The disabled hold a sacred role in Native worldview, a perspective that indeed should undergird these services, not to mention the myriads of medical and care workers that have graduated from tribal colleges that require empowerment. These changes in the ways Native ministries can more properly be ordered to follow an incarnational mission that not only benefits people but also honors and cares for the earth are complex and numerous. May the Creator grant us both the grace and unity to see these changes take place.

34. See Clara Sue Kidwell, Homer Noley, and George E. Tinker, *A Native American Theology* (Maryknoll, NY: Orbis, 2001) 13.

In sum, incarnational and pentecostal mission empowers Native leadership for the mission to Native America. According to the example of the Spirit-empowered Christ, the Christian mission should now defer to Spirit-empowered and Christ-following indigenous Christians in re-conceiving the mission of God among Native peoples. Such an approach to mission seeks to discern how the Logos is and has been the light in every heart (John 1:9) and how the universal Spirit is present and active in order to redeem indigenous cultures for the purposes of the kingdom.[35]

35. Our reflections on this theme are the result of many years of relationships and ministry among the peoples of Latin America and of pastoral work and mission in the Pentecostal churches of North America in contexts of violence, marginalization, poverty, and oppression. These reflections have been further enriched by our years of interaction and dialogue with valuable colleagues at the former Church of God Theological Seminary, now Pentecostal Theological Seminary, in Cleveland, Tennessee, who have helped to open up new vistas for us in contructive Pentecostal theology, especially as it has related to our work and concern for holistic mission. Thanks to many persons and realities which God has placed in our lives through the years. We sense that we have been enriched and fulfilled as persons on mission for and with God, and hope to have been able to contribute in some way to the missionary formation of God's people and to the advancement of missionary consciousness in the churches and educational institutions in which we have been privileged to participate.

# PART FOUR

# Re-Thinking Theology of Mission in a Multifaith World

# 7

# Jamestown and the Future of Mission

## Mending Creation and Claiming Full Humanity in Interreligious Partnership

Shanta Premawardhana

*A new era of the theology of missions is now upon us. Seeking to avoid atrocities such as Jamestown, and the mistakes of the colonial missionary era, this chapter seeks a new methodology that encourages the unique gifts and contributions of each of our religious traditions to create a rich tapestry of our life together. Acknowledging that "mission" is not unique to Christians and drawing upon values that religious people hold in common, the author proposes that Christians engage other religious communities in a conversation about doing mission together. Since such a project requires re-thinking some core concepts, the article questions the meaning and purpose of mission, explores traditional understandings of salvation, seeks to broaden Missio Dei, provides perspective on the politics of identity, and raises a methodological question about "Who is at the table?" These questions are not entirely new. The article draws upon several missiological threads from several twentieth century ecumenical dialogues to locate itself firmly in the ecumenical tradition.*

## INTRODUCTION

IN A STORY FREQUENTLY attributed to him, Rabbi Abraham Joshua Heschel says that when God gets up in the morning the Holy One gathers the angels of heaven around and asks this simple question: "Where does my creation need mending?"[1] Theology, he said, consists of worrying about what God worries about when God wakes up in the morning. It is neither inappropriate nor unusual that a Christian theological reflection begins with the words of a Jewish rabbi, albeit a more contemporary one than the one whose words are normative for us.

A consultation that reflected on the 400 year legacy of Jamestown, Virginia, and its missiological implications then and now was a significant achievement. Initiated by the Virginia Council of Churches, working together with the National Council of Churches of Christ and with the support of the World Council of Churches, the consultation brought a broad range of Christians to Regent University, a bastion of conservative Evangelical Christianity located within reasonable geographical proximity to the original Jamestown settlement. Demonstrating the urgency of these missiological questions for our day and the necessity for such conversations to take place across traditional divides, the consultation succeeded in bringing together a variety of Evangelical and Ecumenical theologians and missiologists including those representing Native American, African American traditions, legal scholars and church leaders for shared reflection. Now with that rich reflection as background, my task is to reflect on the future of mission.

In 2010 the Ecumenical community will celebrate the centenary of a landmark event in the history of Christian Mission and Ecumenism, the World Missionary Conference of Edinburgh. A century ago, when the colonial missionary movement was at its peak, this conference was called to consider the challenges that faced the missionary movement, in particular an unexpected reality it faced in Asia. In the words of F. W. Steinthal, it was the realization that there is "among Hindus and Brahmans as deep, genuine and spiritual religious life as is found among most Christians."[2]

Although this was one of the express concerns, among the 1,200 delegates at that gathering, all but 17 were European or North American.[3] In other words, even though many participants at that event

1. As cited by Marilyn J. Legge, "Inside Communities, Outside Conventions: What is at Stake in Doing Theology?" *Studies in Religion* 29 (2000) 3–18.

2. As quoted in S. Wesley Ariarajah, *Hindus and Christians: A Century of Ecumenical Thought* (Grand Rapids: Eerdmans, 1991) 21.

3. This figure is derived from the statistical data provided in the *World Missionary Conference, 1910, The History and Records of the Conference Together with Addresses Delivered at the Evening Meetings* (New York: Revell, 1910) 18–19.

were involved in missionary activities in foreign lands, the majority did not have an authentic knowledge or experience of living among people of other faiths. Predictably, the conference concluded with an optimistic invitation to churches around the globe to join in the task of evangelizing the world "in our generation." Even though in its early stages the colonialists thought of missionaries as impeding their commercial interests, the missionaries believed that the colonial expansion provided an unprecedented opportunity for evangelization. Later the colonialists too saw the advantage of missionary work in subduing the people in their colonies. Believing that the future of the world and God's cause depended on them, the conference, in its message to the "members of the Church in Christian lands" wrote:

> We have heard from many quarters of the awakening of great nations. Of the opening of long-closed doors, and of movements which are placing all at once before the Church a new world to be won for Christ. The next ten years will in all probability constitute a turning point in human history.... If they are rightly used, they may be among the most glorious in Christian history.[4]

This optimistic statement which celebrates the opportunities for evangelism occasioned by colonization, does not display any awareness of the violence that empire-building caused indigenous populations across the world. The colonization of Jamestown which occurred about 300 years prior to that date decimated the Indigenous Communities in the Americas. As Robert J. Miller amply demonstrates elsewhere in this volume, the infamous "Doctrine of Discovery," a papal edict promulgated by Pope Nicholas V in 1452, legitimized this colonialist violence. To claim that the same doctrine that gave religious legitimacy to the colonizing movement in the Americas did similar damage to Indigenous Communities in Asia and Africa is not a huge step.

Neither did the conference participants realize that they were in the waning days of that empire. Indeed, a few years after the conference, the world plunged into the First World War, heralding the beginning of the end of European hegemony over the world. This was followed in quick succession by the Bolshevik Revolution, marking the triumph of "godless" Marxism. The following decades saw the rise of secularism, scientific advancement, modern culture, and a growing awareness of religious

4. Ibid., 108.

plurality with alternative claims for interpreting reality and alternative centers of transcendence. The century saw the disastrous consequences of fascism, and the horror of the holocaust, which, at least partly, was fuelled by Christian anti-Judaism. Christianity's collusion with racism, imperialism and capitalism was exposed and a generation of young people left the church disaffected by its hypocrisy. At the beginning of the last century, in our eagerness for Christian hegemony, we asked the wrong question: "How can we win the world for Christ?" At the beginning of this twenty-first century, as Christianity's axis has shifted to the global south, and we are aware more than ever before of the breadth of religious diversity around us, I suggest we learn from our older sibling to ask a different question: one that will take us from our self-absorption to engaging with the Creator, "Where does creation need mending?"

That question presented as the starting point for theology, I suggest, is actually a missiological question. Had Heschel's Jewish theological tradition designated an academic discipline separate from theology, he might have said so as well. Missionaries, representatives of the church with their feet on the ground are the ones most attentive to where creation is in need of mending. From the time of the early church, those who were sent on apostolic missions are the ones who raised difficult questions that led to theological grappling with new questions which needed to be resolved through ecclesiastical conferences.[5] When their sensibilities are not blunted by allegiances to colonial or ecclesiastical authorities, missionaries still ask the difficult questions that get the church out of its comfort zones. Asserting, therefore, that this is the right question for a new era in missiological thinking, in this article, I offer brief comments for the consideration of those whose lives and work will impact the future of mission.

## BROADENING THE MEANING AND PURPOSE OF MISSION

The late South African missiologist David Bosch in his *Transforming Mission* describes two sets of eight traditional definitions for the word Mission. The first set, close to its Latin root meaning sending, refers to missionaries being sent and received from, by one part of the world to

---

5. For example, Philip's preaching to the Samaritans in Acts 8, and Peter's encounter with Cornelius, a gentile in Acts 10 among others, leads to the first ecclesiastical council in Jerusalem in Acts 15 and its formative decision about the nature of the church.

another. The second set of meanings refers to the work done by missionaries. All these meanings were set in the missionary context. Before the sixteenth century it was a Trinitarian concept, seen as the sending of the Son by the Father and the Holy Spirit by the Father and the Son. Jesuits, he says, were the first to use it to describe the spread of the Christian faith among people who were not a part of the Catholic Church, and in this sense it was intimately connected with the colonial expansion of the western world. [6] In much of today's Christianity the word is still associated with outmoded colonial images and associations with Christian hegemony. indeed

However obvious, the fact that "mission" is not a Christian word but an English word, must not escape us. Used by governments to describe their diplomatic offices and military adventures, by businesses to describe their core values and goals, the word is also used by Buddhists, Hindus, Jews, Muslims, and those from Indigenous Traditions who also have "missions" and do "missions." Parts of the Christian missionary work, that of establishing schools, hospitals etc. are seen as attractive and appropriate expressions of care for the community, that despite its pejorative connotations the word is in use in non-Christian settings. Since this is the case, the question we need to ask today is: can we, and if so, how can we engage in conversations with our counterparts of other religions about mission, about the values that underlie our engagement in mission, its goals, methods and possible ways of co-operation?

This, of course, is not possible if the missiological conversations are limited to evangelistic strategies, particularly to those that are competitive in tone and substance. Not only Christians, but Muslims, Buddhists, and Hindus have such conversations among themselves. These do not yield to conversations, and certainly not to cooperation, with other religious communities that might be of mutual benefit.

Yet, within all our religions there are strong theological traditions that think of mission more broadly and have the capacity to understand our missiological task in Heschelian terms. If indeed our primary missionary motivation is to find out where creation needs mending, a broader conversation with other religious and even non-religious partners becomes not only possible, but necessary. But for now, even if we confine the con-

---

6. David Bosch, *Transforming Mission: Paradigm Shifts in Theology of Mission* (Maryknoll, NY: Orbis, 1996) 1.

versation of mission to evangelistic activities, I suggest that an interesting conversation is still possible, as the following example demonstrates.

For most Christians, the purpose of mission is to "save" people. They readily quote Matthew 28:19–20 (NRSV): "Go therefore and make disciples of all nations, baptizing them in the name of the Father and of the Son and of the Holy Spirit, and teaching them to obey everything that I have commanded you," which, in the twentieth century has gained greater currency as it has come to be known as the "Great Commission." While Biblical criticism has reliably established that this is a part of the *kerygma* or the preaching of the church, many present-day evangelists have strengthened its appeal claiming this as the charge that Jesus gave his disciples at the end of his life on earth. In addition, by giving it a title they have privileged this text over others that can be more reliably established sayings of Jesus.

An antecedent scripture from an occasion when Jesus sent out his disciples on a mission spells out the content of the teaching: "As you go, proclaim the good news, 'The Kingdom of Heaven has come near.' Cure the sick, raise the dead, cleanse the lepers, cast out demons. You received without payment; give without payment" (Matthew 10:7–8, NRSV). The content of the announcement includes a message of liberation, "The Kingdom of Heaven has come near." The Kingdom of Heaven, where, as a Christian hymn succinctly states, "justice rules with mercy and love is law's demand," stands in sharp contrast to the kingdoms of this world. It is a risky announcement, because while it is good news to the poor and oppressed with whom Jesus closely associated, the Kingdom of Heaven is distinctly bad news to those who oppress and marginalize the poor and the powerless. Also, the announcement is not to be empty rhetoric. It was to go hand in hand with compassionate acts towards those who were sick, in bondage and marginalized from society. And just as the disciples had received this grace freely, they were to give freely.

Like Christians, Buddhists too have a scriptural mandate for propagating their faith. The Buddha commanded the community of disciples thus:

> Go, *bhikkhus,* and wander for the benefit and happiness of the masses, out of compassion for the world, for the welfare, benefit, and happiness of divine beings and humans. Two (of you) are not to go by the same (path). *Bhikkhus,* teach the meaning and detail of the Doctrine that is good in the beginning, good in the middle,

good in the end, fulfilled in its entirety, wholly pure. Make known the holy life. There are those who have few defilements, who are going to ruin through not hearing the Doctrine. They will be the ones who fully understand the Doctrine.[7]

As might be obvious, key elements in these two calls to action are different, but not so dissimilar that we cannot look at them side by side.[8] First, both commissions are given out of a genuine conviction that the message, "the kingdom of heaven has come near," is good news to the poor, and that the "*dhamma* [doctrine], noble in the beginning, in the middle and the end," is for the benefit of people who despite having few defilements, "will go to ruin through not hearing the doctrine." They are clearly intended to lead to salvific ends. Second, the disciples of the Buddha are to go out to the world and teach the *dhamma* "out of compassion for the world" and the disciples of Jesus are not only to announce the kingdom, but they are to engage in compassionate acts on behalf of people. In other words, neither set of disciples is to engage in this work out of a selfish desire to boost numbers for their community or to gain influence.

Since the motivation is compassion and the content of the message is for the benefit of the people, what prevents a conversation between Buddhists and Christians about the purpose, common goals, strategies and methodologies of mission? The problem for Christians is that our missionary motivation has not always been about compassion. It has too often been linked with colonial adventures, and as we have seen in the legacy of Jamestown, it has also been about conquest. The Future of Mission requires deep soul searching and self-critical engagement which takes seriously the motivation with which our Lord calls us to mission: compassion.

There are, of course, examples from other religious traditions as well. But our exploration must move beyond evangelistic endeavors to engaging the Heschelian question. There we will have even more opportunities for cooperative thinking and common action.

---

7. Mahavagga 1.10—11.1 of the Vinaya Pitaka.

8. For an insightful analysis of the two texts see George Soares-Prabhu, "Two Mission Commands: An Interpretation of Matthew 28:16–20 in the Light of a Buddhist Text," in *Voices from the Margin: Interpreting the Bible in the Third World*, ed. R. S. Sugirtharajah (Maryknoll, NY: Orbis, 2002) 319–38.

## RE-THINKING OUR UNDERSTANDING OF SALVATION

A pervasive image in inter-religious circles shows all religions as different paths leading up to the same mountain peak, or as tributaries of a river that leads to the same ocean. S. Mark Heim in his analysis of *Salvations* deconstructs this image, offering instead an image of each religious path leading to its own peak, resulting in an image of many peaks. His point is that the conceptualization of salvation in each religious tradition is unique.[9] However, if each tradition is sitting on top of its own peak, there is no way to dialogue. In order to do that, all have to come down to the valley. The first point I would like to make about this is that the conversation about salvation must not begin at the lofty peaks of theological sophistication or other-worldly imagination, but in the valley, in the midst of real people, and their real concerns.

Soteriology has been a difficult conversation for the Christian ecumenical community. To those with an exclusivistic interpretation, an affirmation that the path to salvation offered by another religious tradition may in any way be true, viable or efficacious is totally unacceptable. Others who prefer a more inclusivistic approach affirm that the life, death and resurrection of our Lord are efficacious for the salvation of all peoples. The pluralistic position which considers the Christian path to salvation as one mountain peak among others, has not found serious currency among most ecumenical churches.

These traditional frames therefore are not the most productive for engaging the Heschelian question. Mending creation, which is fundamentally about healing, however, creates new possibilities. Interestingly, the ecumenical discussions on salvation that have been going on since the 1968 Uppsala Assembly of the World Council of Churches is in recent times changing to include healing.[10]

In the 1968 Uppsala Assembly a consensus based on a more comprehensive rather than the traditional view of salvation seemed to emerge. M. M. Thomas, a strong voice at Uppsala, was a significant contributor to this approach. In his 1971 booklet *Salvation and Humanisation* Thomas

9. S. Mark Heim, *Salvations: Truth and Difference in Religion* (Maryknoll, NY: Orbis, 2003).

10. For a summary of the ecumenical discussion on this subject see Veborn Horsfjord, "Healing and Salvation in Late Modernity: The Use and Implication of Such Terms in the Ecumenical Movement," in *International Review of Mission* 96:380/381 (January/April 2007) 5–21.

captures the essence of the salvation debate in a key phrase in the Uppsala report: New Humanity. Uppsala's description of the mission of salvation, he points out, was the invitation to men and women to put on the New Humanity offered to all by God in the "New Man" Jesus Christ, incarnate, crucified, and risen. The implications of this theological approach, he suggested, "would be that the Mission of the Church must be fulfilled in integral relation to, even within the setting of a dialogue with, the revolutionary ferment in contemporary religious and secular movements which express men's [sic] search for the spiritual foundations for a fuller and richer human life. It is within the context of such a dialogue that proclamation of Christ becomes meaningful."[11]

In 1973, the Commission on World Mission and Evangelism (CWME) meeting in Bangkok gave voice to this new consensus. In its statement "Salvation Today" the Commission wrote:

> Salvation works in the struggle for economic justice against the exploitation of people by people; in the struggle for human dignity against the political oppression of human beings; in the struggle for solidarity against the alienation of person from person; and in the struggle of hope against despair in personal life. In the process of salvation we must relate the four dimensions to each other. There is no economic justice without political freedom, no political freedom without economic justice. There is no justice, no human dignity, no solidarity without hope, no hope without justice, dignity and solidarity. But there are historical priorities according to which salvation is anticipated in one dimension first, be it in the personal, the political or the economic. The point of entry may differ from situation to situation. But we need to realize that such anticipations are not the whole of salvation, and must keep in mind the other dimensions. Forgetting this will deny the wholeness of salvation.[12]

This more holistic approach which encompassed spiritual as well as socio-political aspects in equal measure was reaffirmed at the 1980 meeting of the CWME in Melbourne which reflected on the theme "Your kingdom come." Influenced by Latin American liberation theologies, the conference highlighted the radical aspects of the kingdom message

11. M. M. Thomas, *Salvation and Humanisation* (Madras: CLS, 1971) 4.

12. *Bangkok Assembly 1973: Minutes and Report of the Assembly of Commissions on World Mission and Evangelism of the World Council of Churches, December 31, 1972, and January 9-12, 1973* (Geneva: World Council of Churches, 1973) 88–90.

and the serious challenge it gave to traditional missiology and mission programs. In this conference, the theme of the church as a healing community began to emerge.

However, in the 1980s and 90s the theological mood changed, and for a variety of reasons the ecumenical movement did not follow through on this broad understanding of salvation. I believe it is critically necessary that we pick up from these reflections and re-orient it to reflect contemporary crises. The current financial crisis impacting millions of people across the world, the climate crisis now threatening the existence of several island nations, the food and water crises that are causing riots in many poor countries and the associated crisis of crippling poverty, and interstate and intrastate wars with the resulting massive displacement of people, must be an essential part of the conversation. The affirmations of Bangkok and Melbourne would lead us to understand salvation as the ability to get beyond these dehumanizing conditions, reaching up to our "full humanity."

At the 1996 Salvador, Brazil conference of CWME, the shift towards healing became more evident. Its report includes questions raised by the Christian Medical Commission's evaluation of indigenous spiritualities, whose worldviews are usually more holistic than others, and also possess healing practices usually unavailable to the medical practices of the west. Alternative healing is also being practiced by many Christians in Europe and North America, who are discovering their value through the diversity of religious traditions that have arrived in their societies in the past few decades. In addition, the 2005 Athens conference saw a wide participation of Pentecostal churches. The centrality of healing in Pentecostal faith and practice also pushed the ecumenical movement to take this question seriously.

We already know that like Christians, other religious people also understand the language of "salvation." The word, however, is not directly applicable in other religious contexts, although similar concepts that address emancipation from the human predicament that an individual or community experiences is addressed in most religious traditions. The mission conferences have provided us with two promising starting points for conversation with other communities. If we were to consider the relationship of healing to salvation, that would have exceptional currency within the entire religious world. If we were to consider salvation as reaching up to "full humanity" many non-religious people would be interested in the conversation as well. Since at least one branch of the Christian ecumenical family is on record as affirming these two principles, they provide good starting points for dialogues with other religions, and non-religious communities about common understandings and perceptions of what it means to be saved.

## BEYOND *MISSIO DEI*

Bishop Lesslie Newbigin in his *The Gospel in Pluralist Society* persuasively argues that the phrase "mission of the church" is a misnomer, that there is only God's mission, and that the church is only the vehicle of God's mission.[13] Indeed the question of *Missio Dei* broadened the Christian conversation on mission ever since Karl Barth first proposed it in 1932.[14] Contrary to what Barth and like-minded theologians intended, David Bosch points out that this concept expanded the conversation to include God's activity which "embraces both God and the world and in which the church may be privileged to participate," and which includes places outside the church, persons, communities, and even other religions.[15]

Changing the context from the church's mission to God's mission broadens the parameters of mission. If it is about God's mission then the church cannot discriminate about whom it invites, welcomes and serves. This below-the-surface question has been a difficult one for many churches, who by their structures and practices try to deny participation and thereby restrict God's grace to those beyond certain identity markers. In addition, if it is God's, and not the church's mission, it allows people of many religious traditions to participate in the conversations, contributing their understanding of *Missio Dei* as well. However, if the conversation is to include all religious people, for example Buddhists who have a non-theistic worldview and others who are non-religious, *Missio Dei* ceases to be a useful framing.

M. Thomas Thangaraj, seeking to include all religious and non-religious communities in the conversation on mission, proposes *Missio Humanitatis*,[16] where mission is the work of all human beings taking responsibility, in a mode of solidarity and with a spirit of mutuality. What

13. Lesslie Newbigin, *The Gospel in Pluralist Society* (Grand Rapids: Eerdmans, 1989) 135 ff.

14. Bosch, *Transforming Mission*, 389.

15. Ibid., 391.

16. M. Thomas Thangaraj, *The Common Task: A Theology of Christian Mission* (Nashville: Abingdon, 1999) 47ff.

we usually recognize as the work of the missionary: to go forth from out of him/herself into the world, to return to him/herself to reflectively interpret that world, and then to take responsibility for that world, is also a very normal human activity. Thangaraj sees *Missio Humanitatis* primarily as a way for human beings to take responsibility for ourselves, others, and the world. As in the Cain and Abel story, we do understand ourselves as our brother's/sister's keeper.

The difficulty with responsibility however, is that it carries with it the connotation of doing something *for* others and there are many stories of atrocities committed in the name of those in power doing something for others. For this reason, the acts of responsibility must be undertaken in the mode of solidarity, a notion that recognizes the inter-connectedness and the cohesiveness that needs to exist among people and communities. However, this too is inadequate. *Missio Humanitatis* also includes the notion of mutuality. Unlike in earlier times, where missionary methods required the assumption that the missionary was right and all others were wrong, mutuality recognizes the need for each to learn from the other.

This framing has significant advantages. First, today, people across religious and ideological boundaries, both publicly and privately are engaging in conversations with each other about the issues that affect humanity in general, and their own communities in particular. Second, "mission" has developed into a word in common parlance. Thus the "Human Mission" connotes the possibility that ordinary people might engage in conversations that transcend ordinary selfish concerns that occupy their day to day lives, to engage cooperatively on issues of common concern and enlightened self-interest.

If re-framing mission as *Missio Dei* changed the nature of this Christian conversation, *Missio Humanitatis* has the advantage of being even more inclusive, even of non-religious partners. This framing though, is vulnerable to the critique that it is too anthropocentric. Many religious communities, particularly Indigenous religious communities, who perhaps more than any others understand our interconnectedness with nature and the cosmos, will be quick to offer such a critique.

While Thangaraj's re-framing comes through significant explorations of interconnectedness between religious and non-religious communities, it is still a framing of one Christian theologian. What new insights might we gain, if we engage the other religious communities in this conversation? How would Indigenous Communities frame the question? This is the obvious advantage of having participants of other religions at the table, for they help us to open our eyes to new ways of seeing the same reality.

## THE QUESTION OF IDENTITY

A document produced for the World Council of Churches' 9th General Assembly in February 2006 affirmed that "the 'politics of ideology,' which played a crucial role in the twentieth century, has been replaced in our day by the 'politics of identity.'"[17] This is a critical question when considering the future of mission, particularly in seeking to inter-religiously engage the Heschelian question. The question of identity is, of course, not new to religion, and certainly not to Christianity.

Catherine Keller argues that empires, by which she means not just the western political imperialism of the most recent centuries past, but a variety of systemic dominations by the powers, have used identity to divide and conquer. The church, co-opted by and complicit in the atrocities of the empire, she argues, absorbed the empire's definitions of identity causing it to engage in an *idolatry of identity*.[18]

Indeed, Christian origins point to a vocation far different from that co-opted version. Arising in the midst of a confluence of cultures and in the context of Roman colonization, for its early followers colonial subjugation was not a new experience. The foundational story of its birth affirms the presence of people from across the Roman Empire gathered in Jerusalem for the feast of Pentecost (Acts 2:1–13). The miracle of that day was that the first Christians spoke in the many tongues of nations and cultures of the Empire, leading the disciples to believe that they could communicate across identity markers and beyond boundaries. The story of those first Christians recorded in the book of Acts is a story of breaking through a variety of cultural, linguistic, ethnic, class and religious boundaries to

17. "Religious Plurality and Christian Self-Understanding," preparatory and background paper presented by the programme on Interreligious Relations and Dialogue [as it was called at the time], Commission on World Mission and Evangelism and Faith and Order, to the 9th Assembly of the World Council of Churches, Porto Alegre, Brazil, February 14–23, 2006, §2; available at: http://www.oikoumene.org/en/resources/documents/assembly/porto-alegre-2006/3-preparatory-and-background-documents/religious-plurality-and-christian-self-understanding.html.

18. Catherine Keller "The Love of Postcolonialism," in *Postcolonial Theologies: Divinity and Empire*, ed. Catherine Keller, Michael Nausner, and Mayra Rivera (St. Louis: Chalice, 2004) 221–42.

form a new community mostly comprising those marginalized from civilized society of the Empire—one that included women and slaves. These identities, hardened over centuries to serve the interests of the powerful elites, were softened to create a new identity. Paul's letter to the Galatians describes this community: "There is neither Jew nor Greek, male nor female, slave nor free, for you are all one in Christ Jesus" (Galatians 3:28). For the blurring of these oppressive identities, and the claiming of a liberative identity of a messianic community, the early Christian community was subject to society's derision. Indeed, their new identity "Christian" came to be used derogatorily against them (Acts 11:26).

In three centuries, however, the church had become a part of the Empire. Once inclusive and inviting, the church's identity turned to become like that of the empire, an identity that either excluded or subordinated every "other." Like the society around it, the church too began to think in binary, mutually exclusive expressions of identity that serve the interests of the empire.

In many instances, Christianity's identity hardened as it conflated with national identities. This was particularly the case in Europe. If you lived under the jurisdiction of the British monarch, for example, you were presumed to belong to the Church of England. Indeed you were likely to have been baptized as an infant into the King's church. The pastoral needs of people who lived in a particular geographical area called a parish were attended to by the local vicar, just as the law enforcement needs were attended to by the local constable. Religious and national identity were so conflated that the occasional conversion to a dissenting religious community, particularly to one with Anabaptist roots, was deemed to be so treasonous that some received capital punishment.

Even today, in many countries around the world, the linking of religious, ethnic and national identities continues to pose challenges, complicating many conflicts around the world. For example, the conflict between India and Pakistan is often seen as a Hindu–Muslim conflict and the continuing crises in the Middle East have distinctly religious overtones. The American military and economic involvement in the Middle East is perceived by some to be a Christian intrusion into the heart of the Muslim world. Iranian president Mahmoud Ahmadinejad's rhetoric against Israel is seen as a Muslim threat against Jews. Jews as a religious people are seen as intricately involved with the modern state of Israel and its violence against Palestinians, and the recent Israeli attacks on Gaza are seen as a Jewish war against Muslims. In Sri Lanka, the linking of the Sinhala ethnic identity with the Buddhist religious identity has caused the perceived threat against the Sinhala community by the Tamil militants to be considered a threat to the Buddhist religion such that a political party made up entirely of Buddhist monks is encouraging the government to wage an all out war against the militants.

Media often exacerbates this problem by tending to portray conflicts as religious or religiously motivated when the real causes tend to be either political or economic. Deconstructing conflict and delinking identity conflations therefore become critical questions, not just for Christians but for all religious communities, providing yet another starting point for engaging the Heschelian question.

## WHO'S AT THE TABLE?

That leads us to a critical methodological question for missiology. In light of the foregoing it is clearly arrogant for Christians to think that they can give an adequate answer to the Heschelian question without seeking the wisdom of other religious traditions. While it is true that Christians have for decades related with persons of other religions in dialogue to learn about their neighbor's faith, when it comes to really engaging the other, not just to learn from, but to invite them to grapple together with questions of common mission, Christians have been reluctant. A part of that hesitation arises from the view that only Christians can be recipients of divine revelation and that therefore only they should be consulted.

As we noted earlier, when the World Missionary Conference met in Edinburgh in 1910, "Who's at the table?" was not a question to which the planners paid attention. Another pivotal event in the ecumenical journey, however, the 1938 International Missionary Conference held at Tambaram, South India did have an expanded table, which included many Asian theologians whose lived experience included relating with neighbors and colleagues of other religious traditions.

The assembly's preparatory text, *The Christian Message in a Non-Christian World* written by the Dutch theologian Hendrik Kraemer, using Barthian categories of the uniqueness and decisiveness of the Christian faith, sought to justify the evangelizing mission of the church as universally valid.[19] Revelation became a serious point of the assembly's discus-

---

19. Hendrik Kraemer, *The Christian Message in a Non-Christian World* (London: Edinburgh/International Missionary Council, 1938).

sion. Kraemer framed the question this way: "From the standpoint of the Christian revelation, what answer can be given to the question: Does God—and if so, how and where does God—reveal Himself in the religious life as present in non-Christian religions?"[20] "How do we go about answering this question?" asks Diana Eck, writing about this question fifty years after Tambaram.[21] Who will we ask? With whom will we discuss? To what authority will we turn? Eck continues: "If we want to know what God has been doing in the religious life of Muslims, or what God has revealed of God's self to Hindus, it would seem imperative to ask a Muslim, or a Hindu, 'What have you discovered? What have you seen, or what has been shown to you? What is your struggle?'" In other words, engage Muslims and Hindus in a theological conversation about the content of revelation. But, she points out, despite having lived for years in Indonesia among Muslims, Kraemer does not engage Muslims in this way. When he talks about Islam, the voices of Muslims do not enter. "His method for answering the question, 'Does and, if so, how and where does God reveal himself to Muslims?' is to consult Christian revelation, Christian scripture and Christian theology."[22]

Many, including the Asian theologians at Tambaram speaking from the perspective of their lived experience and expertise of other religious traditions, brought a strong critique and an alternative voice. That voice, however, was drowned out. Despite their bitter complaints, the assembly adopted a statement based on Kraemer's theology which came to be known as the "Tambaram position" as against the Asian theologians' "dialogical attitude." Wesley Ariarajah claims that the repercussions of this dispute were felt for decades after 1938, effectively polarizing the ecumenical movement.[23]

Was the inclusion of the Asian theologians necessary and useful? Were the tensions worthwhile? For some, the inclusion of the Asian theologians, who brought in an alternative perspective to the grand narrative of evangelizing the world, dominant at this table since 1910, was deeply threatening. A derisive designation—the "younger churches"—began to

20. Kraemer, *Christian Message in a Non-Christian World*, 111.

21. Diana L. Eck, "The Religions and Tambaram: 1938 and 1988," *International Review of Mission* 78:307 (1988) 380.

22. Eck, "Religions and Tambaram," 381.

23. Ariarajah, *Hindus and Christians*, 168.

be used on Asian churches, to indicate an immature theological tradition.[24] For others, however, the participation of Asian Christians at the table significantly strengthened the theological discussion, bringing in a previously unheard perspective. It also moved the ecumenical movement in a trajectory that began, however hesitantly, towards taking inter-religious dialogue seriously.

Despite the tensions, which at times have been serious, the ecumenical table has held. The Lund Principle, so called for the city in Sweden in which the Faith and Order movement articulated it in 1952, has characterized this commitment to the ecumenical table: "We will act together in all matters except those in which deep differences of conviction compel us to act separately,"[25] is a statement of strong commitment of the churches to each other, but one that affirms the unique distinctives and differences of the individual communions. In 2005, addressing a gathering of 130 religious leaders, activists, and scholars in a conference in Geneva called "A Critical Moment in Interfaith Dialogue," Dr. Samuel Kobia, the General Secretary of the World Council of Churches made reference to the Lund Principle, suggesting that this principle should now begin to characterize the inter-religious table as well.[26] While the General Secretary's comment is indicative of the progress the ecumenical community has made in this journey, the following example of a programmatic activity describes the possibilities.

Over the past ten years, a small group of 15–20 scholars from five different religions have come together under the auspices of the World Council of Churches to experiment with a process called "Thinking Together." During this time, they have explored Religion and Violence, Theologies of the Other, and currently, Conversion. The scholars, who are all practicing Muslims, Jews, Hindus, Buddhists, and Christians, write papers on a particular facet of the subject and present them to the group for

24. This notion is, of course, absurd given that these supposedly "younger churches" includes the Mar Thoma Church which locates its origins in the ministry of St. Thomas the Apostle.

25. Oliver S. Tomkins, ed., *The Third World Conference on Faith and Order, Lund 1952* (London: SCM, 1952) 15–16.

26. Opening remarks by Rev. Dr Samuel Kobia, World Council of Churches general secretary, June 7, 2005, available at: http://www.oikoumene.org/index.php?id= 1031&MP=935-1037.

peer review. Based on their critique and following robust dialogue, they re-write them in preparation for publication.

Not only does the group grapple with content, it sharply focuses on methodology. Acutely aware of who is at the table and who is not, the group asks questions such as: Is it proper theological method to have colleagues from other religious traditions critique your theology? Or, conversely, is something inadequate or insular about theology that is done without the presence and participation of colleagues of other religions? Since the process is new to each of the religious traditions present at the table, each examines ways in which such questions can be tested within his or her own religious tradition.

## CONCLUSION

The horrific experience of Jamestown 400 years ago must be repudiated with all our strength. Any vestiges of the Doctrine of Discovery which includes colonial attitudes or Christian hegemonic desires must also be rejected. This is possible only when Christians deeply reflect and ask hard self-critical questions about those parts of our self-understanding that led to such atrocities. But we cannot do that by ourselves, since none of us has adequate perspective by ourselves. We need to do that together with our sisters and brothers from the Native Communities and the African American communities, many of whose ancestors entered the United States as slaves through Jamestown.

Such reflection could lead to a new Doctrine of Discovery, one that encourages and enables the discovery of the unique gifts and contributions each of our religious traditions make to the rich tapestry of our life together. It is such recognition that enables the creating of tables of strong commitment for cooperative action.

It is time, therefore, to bring colleagues of many religious traditions and non-religious movements to the table to explore our common concerns that take us beyond ourselves to the outer reaches of our experience, to reflectively interpret those experiences, and then to find ways to work cooperatively to address those concerns. This, I propose, is the way to engage Heschel's divine question: "Where does my creation need mending?"

*important!*

*stop 3 article on Moodle*

8

# Moving beyond Christian Imperialism
# to Mission as Reconciliation with all Creation

WILLIAM R. BURROWS

*In his Regensburger Referat of September 12, 2006, Joseph Ratzinger / Benedict XVI says that some forms of contemporary discussion of incultura- tion are a manifestation of the weaknesses of modern Western relativism. Benedict has no doubt that in Jesus and the gospel there is something abso- lute, unique, and universal that has happened for the benefit of all. The writ- ings of George Tinker, professor of American Indian cultures and religious traditions at Iliff School of Theology, appear to reject the entire heritage of mission and Christian identity based on such notions of universality. This paper will discuss whether there is any commensurable basis for meaningful dialogue between Tinker and the bearers of the Western Christian tradition. And ultimately, can the language of mission derived from that tradition be redeemed?*

## INTRODUCTION

W HEN THE WORDS "JAMESTOWN 1607," "mission," and "implica- tions for 2007 and beyond" are put together, you have landed in the midst of some of the most fought over and controversial terrain in the civil and religious history of the Americas. Jamestown in 1607, of course, was the site of the first permanent colony founded from England in North America. St. Augustine, Florida, however, was established almost fifty years earlier and was the hub of Spanish America north of the Rio Grande for almost two hundred years. Iberian and English imperialism and colonialism—Catholic and Protestant—were different, to be sure, but one must think about mission in "the Americas" as a whole to come to terms with the legacy of Jamestown. Any attempt to make *theological* sense of either mission or the implications of Jamestown 1607 demands a new approach.

## THE PROFOUND AMBIGUITY OF MISSION
## TO NATIVE AMERICANS

The word *mission* has many meanings, but the focal image of the word as used in this paper is the one from the early 1500's through the late 1900's. As I use it here, it refers to organized activities of Christians to spread the gospel of and about Jesus Christ and to establish the Christian church among the indigenous peoples of the Americas. This mission, even when it resulted in some Indians freely embracing Christianity in either its Catholic or Protestant forms and finding fulfillment in it, is so tainted by the Iberian and Anglo-American imperial and colonial projects, that only people with no historical consciousness can view it as anything but ambiguous.[1] In what follows, I presume that ambiguity without arguing the case, basing myself on the scores of books that document Indian-White transactions in the Americas, as Europeans and later Euro-Americans seized the land, using any necessary force or subterfuge to accomplish their goal.

Most of the evangelizing agents were convinced of the notion that *their* truth was the *only valid* "truth" about God and that explicit faith, baptism, and membership in the church were the sole way to obtain not just the promise of the gospel but also the "benefits" of the only civilization that really counted. Indians were viewed mainly as potential converts, not as bearers of worthy traditions in their own right. This conviction led our missionary forebears to allow centuries-old *Christendom* justifications for the use of force to occlude the fundamental *Christic* insights that: (1) the paradigmatic revelation of God and the ways of God are found in the paradoxes of the passion, death, and resurrection of Jesus; (2) that faith is a mysterious reality of existential alignment with Christ much more

1. See Achiel Peelman, *Christ Is a Native American* (Maryknoll, NY: Orbis, 1995) for an excellent account of both the positive and the negative elements in this mission from a Catholic perspective, along with an analysis of the distinctive elements of Indian Christian identity on the part of Indians who identify as Christians (while in many cases continuing simultaneously to follow also the ways of their forefathers and foremothers).

than conceptual beliefs; and (3) that this alignment with Jesus in faith may well be compatible with a lively respect for the traditions of Indians' ancestors and therefore demanded what today would be called respectful intercultural dialogue.

In 1 Corinthians 1:18–19, Paul relies on a paradoxical strand of Hebrew prophetic insight after the Exile to make the cross the central symbol of Christianity. We delude ourselves if we doubt that the church will incur similar judgments when it moves away from its one true foundation, being related to the living God revealed in the relationship of crucified Jesus to God.

## BENEDICT XVI: EVALUATING MISSION IN THE AMERICAS

The speech of Pope Benedict XVI given on 13 May 2007 in Aparecida, Brazil shows, I believe, that he holds a view of mission in the Americas among Native peoples that is out of touch with its ambiguities. Speaking of the results of missions begun 500 years ago the pope says that this encounter, "has animated the life and culture of [the Latin American] nations . . . [from which] has emerged the rich Christian culture of this Continent, expressed in art, music, literature, and above all in the religious traditions and in the peoples' whole way of being, united as they are by a shared history and a shared creed that gives rise to a great underlying harmony, despite the diversity of cultures and languages."[2]

Pope Benedict sees the results of Catholic mission undergoing "serious challenges" today because "the harmonious development of society and the Catholic identity of these peoples are in jeopardy." A careful reader will realize that these challenges refer: (1) to the advance of secularism and the falling away of Latin Americans in the sprawling cities from Christian religious observance and identity; and (2) to the progress that independent Pentecostal and Evangelical churches are making in attracting Catholics to them. As the Pope's address continues, he makes the extraordinary statement, "In effect, the proclamation of Jesus and of his Gospel did not at any point involve an alienation of the pre-Columbian cultures, nor was it the imposition of a foreign culture" (§1). The warrant

2. Pope Benedict XVI, *Address to the Inaugural Session of the Fifth General Conference of the Bishops of Latin American and the Caribbean* (Rome: Libreria Editrice, Vaticana, 2007) §1. Citations from this papal address in the next paragraph will be referred to in text by section number.

for this statement, which caused no little controversy when it was uttered, lies in the Pope's belief that

> Authentic cultures are not closed in upon themselves, nor are they set in stone at a particular point in history, but they are open, or better still, they are seeking an encounter with other cultures, hoping to reach universality through encounter and dialogue with other ways to life and with elements that can lead to a new synthesis, in which the diversity of expressions is always respected as well as the diversity of their particular cultural embodiment. (§1)

The pope is advancing the idea that constant change goes on and that among such changes are the abandonment of one religious tradition in favor of another. The freedom of every religious tradition to be present in every part of the world and to attract as members anyone who wants to join is one of Pope Benedict's constant themes. But he nowhere addresses the question whether the Indian peoples were really given a choice about embracing not just the gospel but the total package of imperialism and colonialism.

It is true that after returning to Rome, Benedict became aware of the controversy his remarks had caused and that in one of his Wednesday allocutions, he showed he was aware that the evangelization of Latin America was more complicated that he had said earlier.

> Certainly, the memory of a glorious past cannot ignore the shadows that accompany the work of evangelization of the Latin American Continent: it is not possible, in fact, to forget the suffering and the injustice inflicted by colonizers on the indigenous populations, whose fundamental human rights were often trampled upon.
>
> But the obligation to recall such unjustifiable crimes—crimes, however, already condemned at the time by missionaries like Bartolomé de Las Casas and by theologians like Francisco de Vitoria of the University of Salamanca—must not prevent noting with gratitude the wonderful works accomplished by divine grace among those populations in the course of these centuries.
>
> The Gospel has thus become on the Continent the supporting element of a dynamic synthesis which, with various facets and according to the different nations, nonetheless expresses the identity of the Latin American People.[3]

3. Pope Benedict XVI, Wednesday Audience, May 23, 2007, available at http://www.vatican.va/holy_father/benedict_xvi/audiences/2007/documents/hf_ben-xvi_aud_20070523_en.html (last accessed June 1, 2009).

That said, the impression left is that it took a public outcry to elicit something closer to the ambiguity of the historical record. The reason for this, I think, is that Pope's ultimate warrant for saying that the adoption of Christianity in the Americas is justified is Christological:

> Christ, being in truth the incarnate *Logos*, "love to the end," is not alien to any culture, nor to any person; on the contrary, the response that he seeks in the heart of cultures is what gives them their ultimate identity, uniting humanity and at the same time respecting the wealth of diversity, opening people everywhere to growth in genuine humanity, in authentic progress. The Word of God, in becoming flesh in Jesus Christ, also became history and culture.[4]

My problem with Pope Benedict's speech at Aparecida is neither with his Christology nor missiology. Rather, it is with the way in which he lets the "Big Truth" of Christology trump the voice of those who, in the words of Tinker's subtitle for his most recent book, have had their cultural and religious "sovereignty," indeed, their very lives, violated.[5]

The question for missiology, as it straddles the ground between the high Christology and missiology of the Bible and tradition, on the one hand, and the voices of those who suffered in the past and their descendants, on the other hand, is this. How should members of the churches that carried on evangelization in the wake of the onslaught of Western imperialism and the campaign to bring new lands and peoples into the global commercial system deal today with the deep ambiguity of Christian mission among the Native Peoples of the Americas?

## GEORGE E. "TINK" TINKER: ANTIPODE TO THE POPE?

If I may briefly characterize the distinguished body of work produced by Professor Tinker—Professor of American Indian Cultures and Religious Traditions at Iliff School of Theology in Denver—over many years,[6] it may be sufficient to make two basic remarks. *First*, there is the critical moment

4. Pope Benedict XVI, *Address to the . . . Bishops of Latin American and the Caribbean*, §1.

5. George E. "Tink" Tinker, *American Indian Liberation: A Theology of Sovereignty* (Maryknoll, NY: Orbis, 2008).

6. Two of the books Tinker is best known for are: *Political Theology and American Indian Liberation* (Minneapolis: Fortress, 2004), and *The Gospel and Native American Cultural Genocide* (Minneapolis: Fortress, 1993).

in his work—the demand that Euro-Americans recognize the injustice of their imperial project and its effects on the Indians. In this area, he would have serious problems with the Pope or anyone else justifying in any straightforward manner what has developed out of the five centuries of Christian mission. This would go for both Latin America and for North America. Tinker has an unerring instinct for the way in which missions in North America attempted to stamp out Native American traditions that they almost uniformly viewed as idolatrous. They did so even though few of the missionaries knew the languages, the meaning of the rituals and practices, the wisdom, and the worldviews that these traditions embodied well enough to make an informed judgment in such matters.

At another level, the crimes go on. The first that Tinker points out raises the issue of what the treatment of Indians has done to them as a people and as individuals. In a particularly moving section in *American Indian Liberation*, Tink relates the impact on him of the death of his *hunka* "brother" (who, he says, "was closer than flesh and blood") who died of a mixture of alcohol and anti-depressant drugs. But in healthier days he was also the force behind the Living Waters Indian Ministry and its successor organization, Four Winds Indian Council, while he himself was merely the front man. As a child, though, his brother was taken by Bureau of Indian Affairs police to a church mission school and baptized by a priest whose true initiation was not into the Christian faith but into "the evil realities of Indian domination by Whites, of child domination by adults, of the domination of individual self-gratification in a White world way."[7] The priest also raped his brother's friend, Clifford, who would die a suicide at seventeen. The treatment of his brother stands as a metaphor for the way in which Indian peoples both were and still are treated.

*Second*, there is a constructive element to Tinker's work. Wary of trendy White attempts to borrow superficially from Indian religious traditions and practices to provide a dance and a drum beat for a church meeting, he also wants to retrieve the authentic traditions of his people and help Native peoples re-appropriate them, both because these practices help them recognize the spiritual forces that permeate the world and participate experientially in their reality. In so doing, they lead Indians in coming to terms with an Indian identity that they have been led away from. In Tinker I see profound belief that these spiritual forces are real

7. Tinker, *American Indian Liberation*, 153.

and beneficial. His is not merely instrumentalizing traditional religion to attain political goals. Instead he teaches that truly *human* beings live in harmony with these forces and discover a deeper truth and peace that Westernized Christianity does not communicate. At another level, aware of the negative self-images that Indian peoples have imbibed from White culture, these powers help a generation alienated both from their own religious and cultural traditions and those of White America appreciate the depths, the authenticity, and the riches of the Indian Way. This will entail the necessity of Whites recognizing their whiteness and finding a way to their own spiritual center and for Indian realization that Indian "liberation is not possible without the liberation of our White relatives who share this continent with us [Indians]."[8]

What Tinker's *American Indian Liberation* drove home to me is the profound misreading so many Whites make when they think of Native American Religion as primarily analogous to private spirituality in the modern American sense. Tinker's subtitle, however, speaks of "a theology of sovereignty." Indian religious identity is not merely a set of beliefs, it is a total way of life bound to "reciprocity and space." When land is stolen, the very basis of a life in which reciprocity between human beings and the land that is inhabited by various invisible forces is destroyed.[9] We shall return to the implications of this truth at the end of this discussion.

*Third,* Tinker is utterly disdainful of any attempt to hide the magnitude of the cultural and physical genocide that the invaders nearly succeeded in perpetrating. He is skeptical whether Christianity is compatible with the Indian Way. Minimally, his attention has turned to reacquainting his people with the ways of their ancestors that he judges were in far greater harmony with the rhythms of the universe than contemporary Christian Ways. Tinker is about retrieving Indian traditions in their integrity and helping his people find harmony with God and the world through them. But restoring *real* sovereignty over the land is key to all this.

## TWO MISSIOLOGICAL PRINCIPLES FOR OUR AGE

The missiology of sixteenth through twentieth century North American Christianity fit nicely within the ideology of "manifest destiny" and served well to provide its chaplains with the sense that their mission to

8. Ibid., 141.

9. Ibid., 70–83.

the Indian was part of God's plan for his White people to populate the continent and confer the benefits of a purified American Christianity on the First Peoples. In what follows, I want to suggest a different way of viewing mission after Jamestown.

In 1993 I wrote concluding reflections for a book that collected two late twentieth-century Roman Catholic documents on mission and on proclamation of the gospel in relationship to dialogue with other religions. For Pope John Paul II, I noted, the core mission as the attempt "to share the church's experience of life in Christ across the boundary of faith"—John Paul II's way of expressing the missionary ideal.[10] Over against a practice of mission in which Christianity was too often promoted by missioners who were the chaplains of an imperial project, mission today is sharing faith with another construed as an equal.

John Paul II's *Redemptoris Missio* was written to counteract creeping relativist tendencies doctrines. Benedict XVI fully supports the thrust of his predecessor's message. The style of both, however, betrays an attitude that tries to keep missionary ideals above the fray in a level of theological principle that does not reflect the ambiguities of mission on the ground. In the conclusion to *Redemption and Dialogue*, I went on to say: "If the dynamic of finding new life through death is the ultimate paradigm of Christian existence, then perhaps the death of Jesus is key to a Christian hermeneutic of mission in the contemporary world."[11]

I have gradually been persuaded of two points on which Martin Luther was magisterially clear. The first is that the central issue at stake in the gospel is *God's promise to treat those who embrace Jesus Christ as Jesus himself was treated when he embraced the promise.* The good news of the gospel *is* this promise. It is not a higher morality or a new law, it is a promise embodied in a person. Embracing the One who embodies the promise puts us not so much in the safe world of nature and grace as in the interpersonal word of sin and forgiveness.

The second point follows directly from first. The meaning of the gospel is summed up nowhere as clearly as it is in the cross. As messiah, Jesus is sent to renew Israel by bringing God's people to trust the One whose word is central to the Scriptures, teachings that are much more narratives

---

10. William R. Burrows, "Concluding Reflections," in *Redemption and Dialogue: Reading* Redemptoris Missio *and* Dialogue and Proclamation, ed. William R. Burrows (Maryknoll, NY: Orbis 1993) 239–44.

11. Burrows, "Concluding Reflections," 243.

about a relationship—between God and Israel, God and Jesus, God and the people who follow the promptings of the Spirit to put on Christ—than a belief in doctrines. But we live not in a world that is neutral and simply a matter of original blessing. Instead, the execution of Jesus constitutes a revelation of a form of the human blindness that prefers dwelling in darkness rather than embracing light.

In speaking of a *missiologia crucis*, let it be clear that I am not speaking of issuing new documents or writing better books. I am talking about a bold humility whose authenticity comes from inner conversion to the Spirit of Christ who becomes alive in a church that seeks to bear witness to God's promise revealed in the cross and resurrection. In the context of our discussion of Christian-Indian dialogue, the demand for a profound transformation of Western Christianity could not be more clear.

In Benedict XVI's words to leaders from various Christian churches in New York City on 18 April 2008, the pope advances the notion that Christianity is so divided both because of a mutual rivalry expressed in "prophetic actions" that tend to distinguish and divide the communities from "communion with the Church in every age," and because of "a relativistic approach to Christian doctrine similar to that found in secular ideologies."

Benedict is speaking of Christian disunity, but his principles can be applied to present-day missiology in the wake of Jamestown. If Christian unity is to be found in returning to the Christic principle, so Christian mission *in its dialogic aspect* must flow from that principle. The aim of mission is the creation of a people that mirrors the reconciling justice and love of God and helps bring unity to a world divided by sin. It is this principle that Robert Schreiter embraces in suggesting that "reconciliation" ought to be a primary model for mission.[12] Basic to this is the fact that the ground for reconciliation in history has already been already laid by Christ and that "we"—for example, Indian and White—have the possibility of recognizing and embracing it and *in so doing may become a new creation*. Schreiter encapsulates his message most accessibly in his

---

12. Robert J. Schreiter, "Reconciliation as a Model of Mission," *Neue Zeitschrift für Missionswissenschaft* 52:4 (1996) 243–50; see also Schreiter's "The Theological Meaning of a Truly Catholic Church," *New Theology Review* 7 (1994) 5–17; and *The New Catholicity: Theology between the Global and the Local* (Maryknoll, NY: Orbis, 1997).

book *The Ministry of Reconciliation: Spirituality and Strategies.*[13] I call this process a *missiologia reconciliationis,* a "missiology of reconciliation."[14]

Most books on reconciliation speak of the need for an offending party to wake up to the wrong he or she has done and then to ask for forgiveness. Schreiter's view of the New Testament's vision of reconciliation is somewhat different. In regard to standard human reconciliation strategies, Schreiter notes that they revolve around trying to overcome the results of unjust actions, yet, "While we may overcome these situations, we seem never to be liberated completely; a residue of that violence and oppression has seeped into our bones. The structures we build to replace those from which we were liberated, never quite get it right."[15] In the critical section of his earlier book on the subject, he shows that getting it right entails recognition of five steps:[16]

1. God initiates and brings about reconciliation.

2. Reconciliation is more a spirituality than a strategy.

3. Reconciliation makes both victim and victimizer a "new creation."

4. The story of Jesus' passion, death, and resurrection overcomes the "narrative of the lie" that keeps the truth concealed.

5. Reconciliation is a multidimensional reality.

The classic biblical text is in First Corinthians:

> If someone is in Christ, there is a new creation . . . All this is from God, who reconciled us to himself through Christ, and has given us the ministry of reconciliation; that is, in Christ God was reconciling the world to himself, not counting their trespasses against them, and entrusting the message of reconciliation to us. So we are ambassadors for Christ, since God is making his appeal through us; we entreat you on behalf of Christ, be reconciled to God. (1 Corinthians 5:17–21)

13. Robert J. Schreiter, *The Ministry of Reconciliation: Spirituality and Strategies* (Maryknoll, NY: Orbis, 1998).

14. I expand on this model in my article "Reconciling All in Christ: The Oldest New Paradigm for Mission," *Mission Studies* 15:29 (1998) 79–98.

15. Schreiter, *Reconciliation: Mission and Ministry in a Global Church* (Maryknoll, NY: Orbis, 1993) 59.

16. Ibid., 59–62.

At this point, missiology needs to decide whether mission is a process of entering into the mystery of God, the revealing of whom occurs (as in the Emmaus story, Luke 24:13–32) when one walks with a stranger and recognizes Jesus in the breaking of bread. The fundamental conflict between liberal modernity attempting to explicate Scripture and Indian Religious Ways, on the one hand, and either Pope Benedict or George Tinker doing the same is deep. But at about this point, I suspect that Benedict and Tinker—were they to sit together for a long time—would discover they are in profound agreement about the depths of the conversion needed.

A *missiologia reconciliationis* is about recognizing that we are alienated from the very ground of our being if we do not existentially dwell in, participate in, and trust in God's revelation, presence, and promise. Mission after Jamestown needs to learn from the voices of those who have been hurt by mission fashioned on Christendom principles. Moreover, if Tinker is right, as I think he is, Christians in contemporary industrial societies have much to learn from Indians and other followers of "local religions." Namely, that truly *human* beings live in harmony with the forces and discover a deeper truth and peace that Westernized Christianity does not communicate.

Achiel Peelman quotes Pope John Paul II, during his visit to the Shrine of the Canadian Martyrs in Midland, Ontario, saying, ". . . Christ in the members of his Body is himself Indian."[17] Peelman's book is an exhaustive study of the inculturation of Christianity in Indian Christianity. The one impression I was most clearly left with after Orbis published it was this: *It is up to Indian voices to testify what they have found in Christ . . . if anything.* But I also wondered whether the rationalized, White Western Christian is capable of hearing it. Peelman ends his book with the following words:

> The cultural language of the Amerindians is the language of the human heart and of the intuitive mind. Therefore, it is also a universal language. To the extent that the native peoples of North America are invited to speak this language freely within the Christian churches, the entire Christian community will be better

---

17. John Paul is quoted in Peelman, *Christ is a Native American*, 13; the original quotation is from the *Canadian Catholic Review* 2:9 (1984) 368.

prepared to visualize all the dimensions of the universal Christ mystery.[18]

Whites have done most of the talking for five hundred years in the Americas. It won't hurt to be still. We may discover that another thing Peelman mentions on the same page is also true. The Indian approach is experiential, and they "will not speak of an Amerindian Christ unless they have met, heard or personally experienced him in their lives." That might not be a bad strategy for the rest of us. A *missiologia reconciliationis* requires much more than words. It requires existential participation in the Mystery of God and the willingness for God to bring about a new creation where till now there has been enmity.

The hardest thing for us Whites to realize, I suspect, is that reconciliation with Indians means taking seriously Tinker's assertion that Indian sovereignty has been trammeled and that Indian identity is rooted in a sovereignty over space and land that Westerners are incapable of seeing as anything but a source of minerals, food, or recreation. Christic life begins in repentance and conversion, and White-Indian dialogue in the shadow of the cross demands more than mere good will. Accordingly, a conversation between Pope Benedict and Professor Tinker, I suspect, has to go deeply into humanity's embeddedness in creation and break out of a view of what happens in Christ is mainly about spiritual transformation and eschatological hope.

18. Peelman, *Christ is a Native American*, 226.

# Conclusion

# The Missiology of Jamestown—
# 1607–2007 and Beyond

*Toward a Postcolonial Theology of Mission in North America*

Amos Yong

W E NEED TO CONTINUE to seriously consider the "hard questions" that have been raised in the preceding pages. In this concluding reflection, I want to engage these questions at two levels—the theological and the missiological—and then sketch in response what a postcolonial theology of mission might look like in North America in the twenty-first century.

## THEOLOGICAL QUESTIONS AFTER JAMESTOWN

There are many difficult issues that are discussed in the chapters in this volume. I will begin by noting one of the overarching concerns: that concerning the Christian story considered as a meta-narrative. By using this term, I am intentionally engaging debates occasioned by the post-modern "incredulity toward metanarratives."[1] While I am sympathetic to the counterargument that insofar as the Christian story is based on a faithful reception of the ancient Israelite and apostolic witness it is unlike the metanarratives based on universal reason that have been rejected by

---

1. Most prominently propounded by Jean-François Lyotard, *The Postmodern Condition: A Report on Knowledge,* trans. Geoff Bennington and Brian Massumi (Minneapolis: University of Minneapolis Press, 1984) esp. xxiv.

postmodern thinkers,[2] from another perspective, no hard and fast lines can be drawn between the two since the perpetuation of even faith-based narratives must be amenable to reason and, further, the big-picture of the Christian story has always had missionary impulses that have inevitably engaged aliens and strangers to the Hebraic and Hellenistic Greek ways of life. Yet it is precisely this missionary character of the Christian story that is problematized in light of the history of mission before, during, and after Jamestown.

Most problematic is that intertwining of the Christian story and both the Doctrine of Discovery and the Manifest Destiny impulse of the colonial American experience and the nation's westward expansion. As rendered with stark clarity by both Robert Miller and Edward Bond, both sets of ideas were shot through with Christian motifs and rationalizations. In fact, both were predicated fundamentally on the Christian missionary enterprise itself, and were understood in part as the unfolding of the Great Commission to take the gospel to the ends of the earth. I am certainly not denying that there were also other ideological factors involved in their articulation and implementation. But we cannot minimize or ignore how the Discovery and Destiny doctrines were intertwined with the Christian self-understanding of how their story would continue to unfold in the New World. In other words, it is difficult now to simply say these were aberrations in the history of Christianity; rather, they were self-consciously promulgated as legitimate and even necessary theological expansions of the Christian narrative which was destined to conquer the world.[3]

Of course, the problem is that Christian Europeans ran into a recalcitrant indigenous population. Setting aside the issues of land ownership, the quest to secure resources, and other deeply troubling aspects of the European encounter with Native America,[4] there was also the chal-

---

2. For an articulate defense of this view, see James K. A. Smith, *Who's Afraid of Postmodernism? Taking Derrida, Lyotard, and Foucault to Church* (Grand Rapids: Baker, 2006) ch. 3.

3. That this discover-and-conquer-destiny is tied in with the main strands of the biblical narrative is aptly delineated in Robert Allen Warrior, "A Native American Perspective: Canaanites, Cowboys, and Indians," *Christianity and Crisis* 49 (1989) 261–65, reprinted in R. S. Sugitharajah, ed., *Voices from the Margins: Interpreting the Bible in the Third World* (Maryknoll, NY: Orbis, 1995) 277–85.

4. As one popular textbook puts it, the colonial mission to Native America was motivated by the pursuit of "gold, glory, and God," in that order; see James T. Baker, *Religion in America: Primary Sources in U.S. History*, 2 vols. (Belmont, CA: Wadsworth, 2006) I.6.

lenge of introducing Christian monotheism to the Native inhabitants. Here, Barbara Mann points to the clash of worldviews underneath the confrontation. In her analysis, Christianity's One-Thinking was fundamentally incommensurate with Native Two-Thinking. While some may contest either Mann's association of monotheism with One-Thinking or her incommensurability thesis, or others may counter that Mann's Two-Thinking worldview actually has re-constructed the "other" (the European Christian) within the framework of its own binary terms, there is no disputing that the Christian missionaries were faced with serious theological challenges in their mission to Native Americans. Even if Mann's claim is too strong that Christian and Native ways of thinking are "incompatible paradigms," it is important to acknowledge that not many Christian missionaries seriously undertook the effort to enter into the Native way of life on its terms; that few if any valued Native culture and spirituality in comparison to what the missionaries had to offer; and that it was well nigh impossible for the missionaries to critically re-examine their modern, western, and European assumptions from the various indigenous perspectives. The result, to put it bluntly, following Tinker, was the "cultural genocide" of Native America, legitimated theologically by doctrines like that of Discovery and Destiny.[5]

Might there be a way forward theologically after Jamestown and its horrendous history? Is it possible to retrieve and redeem the Christian story in light of the "failed encounter" (Mann) between Christianity and Native America? Richard Twiss' chapter undertakes some first steps in this direction, albeit with great trepidation. As a member of the Lakota/Sioux Tribe, Twiss wrestles deeply with what it means to be a Native American and Christian. The latter dimension of his identity affirms his relationship with Jesus the Christ. But how is Twiss able to embrace this confession, given the long history of genocide conducted against his people in the name of Jesus?[6] Twiss' proposal is to connect with Jesus as "an aboriginal boy" in the midst of Empire, one who therefore can empathize with the plight of Native Americans at the hands of their colonial conquerors.

---

5. George E. Tinker, *Missionary Conquest: The Gospel and Native American Cultural Genocide* (Minneapolis: Fortress, 1993).

6. Chapter 4 of George E. "Tink" Tinker's *American Indian Liberation: A Theology of Sovereignty* (Maryknoll, NY: Orbis, 2008), explicates the challenges confronting the articulation of a Native American christology.

At one level, one can respond to Twiss' aboriginal christology by simply understanding it as an attempt at theological contextualization or indigenization. Thus Native American perspectives on the Jesus story naturally highlight the parallels between the life of Christ and the contemporary horizon, perhaps an allowable correlation given the biblical insistence that Jesus "had to become like his brothers and sisters in every respect" (Heb 2:17a; NRSV). Yet at a deeper level, note that Twiss must necessarily reach over the historical mediations of Christ through the church, and that in effect, he arrives back at a more primordial Jesus, a cosmic and universal Jesus who is capable of meeting the people of Native America not on the terms of those who originally introduced him, but on indigenous terms. To be sure, as an evangelical follower of Jesus, Twiss is committed to the portrait presented by the gospel evangelists; however, his re-portrayal of the tribal Jesus is rather far afield from how Jesus is understood in White American evangelicalism.

At a third level, however, I suggest that Twiss' approach is more the theological norm than the exception in that it emphasizes the agency of recipients of the gospel message.[7] Each people, as well as each generation, will need to meet Jesus on their terms, rather than on the terms of the missionaries or of their parents.[8] I would go further to claim that this is a legitimate expansion of the incarnational principle: that the Christian conviction that the Word became flesh means not only that Jesus came as a first century Mediterranean Jew, but also that the Word continues to meet all peoples and individuals where they are at. Later on, I will suggest

7. This is in contrast to the view that Native Americans were coerced into or passive digesters of the missionary message. For accounts of Native agency in fashioning the Christian religion for their own (important) purposes, see Nicholas Griffiths and Fernando Cervantes, eds., *Spiritual Encounters: Interactions between Christianity and Native Religions in Colonial America* (Lincoln: The University of Nebraska Press, 1999). A specific case study is provided by Neal Salisbury, "'I Love the Place of My Dwelling': Puritan Missionaries and Native Americans in Seventeenth-Century Southern New England," in *Inequality in Early America: Encounters with Colonialism: New Perspectives on the Americas*, ed. Carla Gardina Pestana and Sharon V. Salinger, (Hanover, NH: University Press of New England, 1999) 111–33.

8. That people inevitably receive the gospel on their own terms in some respects is more clearly seen in anthropological research that specifically asks about indigenous or Native viewpoints regarding their conversion experiences; see, e.g., Aparecida Vilaça and Robin M. Wright, eds., *Native Christians: Modes and Effects of Christianity among Indigenous Peoples of the Americas*, Vitality of Indigenous Religions series (Burlington, VT: Ashgate, 2009).

that when combined with a pentecostal and pneumatological principle, this view does not succumb to philosophical relativism but instead underwrites the universal relevance of the gospel.

## MISSIOLOGICAL PROSPECTS AFTER JAMESTOWN

For the moment, however, I want to turn from theological (and christological) issues to specifically missiological ones. To cut to the chase, the major question before us in light of this history of mission to Native American before, during, and after Jamestown is this: whither the Christian mission? In his chapter, Tink Tinker puts it forcefully thus: "Given the disastrous history of euro-western mission practices—to the cultures and the peoplehood of those missionized—it would seem that there are no missioloigical projects that we might conceive that would have legitimacy of any kind." Recall that Tinker's concerns are informed by the history of Christian aggressions against Native America that have been recounted by him and many others. If some might think that things are better now in the late modern world, Tinker would retort that an even more insidious form of colonialism is currently afoot, one that engages in the ongoing "colonialism of the mind" by continuously communicating the inferiority of the Native American way of life in contrast to the modern, western Christian one.[9] So from this perspective, it is not *how* the mission to Native America should proceed, but *whether* such should proceed at all. The response is: No! Ongoing calls for the conversion of Native Americans perpetuate the Christian quest to eradicate indigenous cultures, and there is no time to be idle in the face of such threats.

On the one hand, of course, Tinker is aware that such a stark response is simplistic in view of the complexities of the interface between Native Americans and the Christian America. On the other hand, however, it would also be a mistake to undertake the Christian mission as usual, as if reparations have now been made, as if healing and reconciliation either already has begun or is in the wings. Sure, there have been tremendous

---

9. Confirmation for Tinker's claim comes from those quite unconnected to his project. See, for example, Jay S. F. Blossom, "Evangelists of Destruction: Missions to Native Americans in Recent Film," in *The Foreign Missionary Enterprise at Home: Explorations of North American Cultural History*, ed. Daniel H. Bays and Grant Wacker (Tuscaloosa: University of Alabama Press, 2003) 237–50, whose analysis of four contemporary films on the Christian mission to Native America uncovers the ongoing agenda to undermine the indigenous worldview and way of life.

strides made in Native American-Christian relations, but there remains much difficult work to be done.

Missiologists Rick Waldrop and Corky Alexander both realize the enormity of the task in light of the specifically pentecostal mission to Native America. The ignominious history of mission after Jamestown has been exacerbated by the zealousness of pentecostal missions in the twentieth century precisely because of sectarian pentecostal attitude toward culture. The outworking of this in the pentecostal missionary enterprise has been a devaluation of things Native, a rhetoric that has intensified the colonial attack on indigenous culture, and a set of conversion practices that have demanded a rejection of many, if not most, traditional forms of life.[10]

Waldrop and Alexander thus struggle to reformulate pentecostal missiology in light of this "failed encounter." Their approach is to emphasize the trinitarian character of God's mission, especially as marked by the incarnation and Pentecost. Their intuitions are headed in the right direction, even if both aspects of their proposal can be made more explicit with regard to the challenge of mission to Native America today. First, the incarnation marks God's entry into human history in all of its specificities, including the diversity that constitutes this history of Native America. Second, the Spirit of Pentecost is also the Spirit who hovered over the primordial creation, and hence has already been present to the peoples of Native America, perhaps is even preserved in its myths and stories. But Waldrop and Alexander could have gone further to retrieve the indigenous principle at the heart of historic pentecostal missiology and to call for its more rigorous and intentional application in the Native American case.[11] The performance of such a pentecostally and pneumatologically informed indigenous principle would have invited Native Americans to receive the gospel on their own terms, or, to put it in more specifically pentecostal language, in their own tongues.[12]

---

10. As documented by Kirk Dombrowski, *Against Culture: Development, Politics, and Religion in Indian Alaska* (Lincoln: University of Nebraska Press, 2001).

11. I discuss this in my *The Spirit Poured Out on All Flesh: Pentecostalism and the Possibility of Global Theology* (Grand Rapids: Baker, 2005) 123–24.

12. We are beginning to see Native articulations of the gospel on their own terms— e.g., James Treat, ed., *Native and Christian: Indigenous Voices on Religious Identity in the United States and Canada* (New York: Routledge, 1996).

Yet as Waldrop and Alexander acknowledge, the success (or not) of the pentecostal missionary venture will have to be measured in the kinds of practices, structures, and relations the come out of the Christian encounter with Native America. This now touches on Tinker's suggestion that what really will count in the future of Christian mission is not so much the proclamation of the gospel but the embodiment of the message of Jesus as peace, justice, and love. Shanta Premawardhana and William Burrows thus both emphasize a more praxis-oriented missiology of reconciliation designed to live rather than just preach Christ. Premawardhana's emphasis, following the Asian Indian Christian theologian, M. M. Thomas, is on the *missio humanitatis*, highlighting the central role of humanization as the goal of mission. This is certainly in keeping with the major themes that have unfolded in the last century of mainline Protestant missiologies. Deeply aware of the problematic 400-year history of Jamestown, the ecumenical churches have tended to thoroughly reconsider the nature of the Christian mission. Premawardhana's description of joint mission captures the partnership aspect of the ecumenical approach involving collaboration on goals related to human flourishing and well-being. There is much to be said about such a missiological proposal. And even if the ecumenical reluctance to be offensive to non-Christians tends to produce a bland all-inclusive gospel, it is nevertheless important for us not to quickly forget the offenses that were part and parcel of the missiology of Jamestown.

So, if Mann (explicitly) and Tinker (at least on the surface) call for the withering of mission in light of the history of Jamestown, read more deeply, I think we can say that Tinker (in his own way), along with Waldrop, Alexander, Premawardhana, and Burrows each ask instead, Whither the Christian mission? It is safe to say that none of the Christians in this volume deny the essentially missionary character of their faith; yet the question after Jamestown concerns the *how* of this mission going forward. Each is concerned about the integrity of the Native American side of the encounter. Is there a way to craft a "missiology after Jamestown" that preserves the Native American voice and perspective on theological rather than merely politically correct grounds?

## TOWARD A POSTCOLONIAL THEOLOGY OF MISSION
## IN NORTH AMERICA

In effect, what we are searching for can be understood as a postcolonial theology of mission for the specifically North American context.[13] I would like to propose for consideration what is hinted at but undeveloped in Waldrop and Alexander's and Twiss' chapters: a robustly trinitarian theology of mission particularly because of a thoroughly pentecostal and pneumatological emphasis.[14] Such an approach is consistent with the incarnational and trinitarian model they present, but the pneumatological dimension is not just subsumed within the broader theological framework. Rather, the pneumatological trajectory opens up substantive theological space for rethinking Christian missionary praxis in ways that are consistent with a postcolonial emphasis on Native American agency and perspective. Let me flesh out five aspects of such a postcolonial and pneumatological theology of mission for twenty-first century North America.

First, a postcolonial and pneumatological theology of mission draws fundamentally from the many tongues of the Pentecost narrative. As many languages were empowered by the Spirit to speak about God's deeds of power on that day (Acts 2:11), so also are many languages required to bear witness to the glory of God today. Such a pentecostal theology of mission thus requires attentiveness to the diversity of testimonies that characterize the life of humankind. Testimonies are, after all, the most powerful forms of religious proclamation. Richard Twiss's more or less autobiographical theological reflections are effective precisely because they emerge out of his own journey in search for a tribal or aboriginal Jesus.[15] But the wildness and weirdness of the many tongues of Pentecost also suggest that

13. My use of the notion of "postcolonial" is shorthand for "after Jamestown." For initial articulations of a postcolonial missiology in an Asian context, see Jacob S. Dharmaraj, *Colonialism and Christian Mission: Postcolonial Reflections* (Delhi: Indian Society for Promoting Christian Knowledge, 1993).

14. I have written extensively about pneumatological theology. For my most recent and sustained attempt to elaborate a pneumatological theology of mission in a pluralistic world, see Yong, *Hospitality and the Other: Pentecost, Christian Practices, and the Neighbor* (Maryknoll, NY: Orbis, 2008).

15. For a booklength argument regarding the centrality of testimonial biography and autobiography to religious proclamation and even theological formulation, see James William McClendon Jr., *Biography as Theology: How Life Stories Can Remake Today's Theology* (Nashville: Abingdon, 1974).

when we encounter testimonies that fit only with difficulty or even not at all—like those of Barbara Mann's—with those we feel called to perpetuate we may need to be especially attentive rather than to refuse to listen. We cannot simply reject, silence, or neglect such uncomfortable voices since they bear witness to truths that we ignore to our own detriment.

Of course, discerning exactly what is true is complicated (as complicated as is discerning the truths of Twiss' testimony), but we cannot proceed to discernment apart from first listening. This leads to my second point: that the many tongues of Pentecost presume the importance of listening to the many voices. Here I wish to expand William Burrows' proposal for a *missiologia crucis* in a pneumatological direction. If Burrows highlights the centrality of a humble missiology based on the cross of Christ (rather than a triumphalist missiology based only on the resurrection), I would further emphasize that such humility attempts to follow the winds of the Spirit who has been poured out upon all flesh (Acts 2:17) and thus potentially is capable of speaking through the many strange tongues of others. In practice, this means that in the initial encounter, we efface ourselves in humility before (religious) others. Missiologists Terry Muck and Frances Adeney talk about this in terms of bracketing our convictions (and especially prejudices) sufficiently in order to be able to sympathetically listen to, interact with, and maybe even experience another language, culture, and religious tradition.[16] Such bracketing is absolutely imperative for a postcolonial theology of mission in light of Jamestown.[17]

Of course, such bracketing is only an initial moment in the encounter, and it is questionable whether it can really be achieved. But, and this is my third point, such bracketing is grounded incarnationally and pentecostally (pneumatological) in the work of God who has really entered human history. Thus God achieves the conversion of humanity but not before emptying himself in Christ and pouring out of himself in the Spirit. Hence any evaluation and assessment of the religious other—always necessary and unavoidable moments of the interreligious encounter—in the postcolonial theology of mission I am proposing always already presumes some

16. See Terry Muck and Frances S. Adeney, *Christianity Encountering World Religions: The Practice of Mission in the Twenty-First Century* (Grand Rapids: Baker, 2009) esp. Part 3.

17. I have also previously called for a bracketing of theological convictions for purposes of forestalling imperialistic approaches and of allowing religious others to be present to us first on their own terms; see Yong, *Beyond the Impasse: Toward a Pneumatological Theology of Religions* (Grand Rapids: Baker, 2003) esp. ch. 7.

kind conversion toward the other in and through the encounter. This mutual conversion is most aptly illuminated by Twiss' aboriginal christology as such involves both a transformation of Christian and Native identities simultaneously. Of course, such a mutual transformation will be rejected either by those (conservative Christians) who deem such as syncretism or by others (Native Americans who remain suspicious of Christianity) who see such as a disguised form of imperialism. While there is no way to qualm the fears of either side (since syncretism and imperialism always remain real possibilities), I am optimistic such a postcolonial and pneumatological theology of mission allows for a healthy tension that takes seriously the task of reinterpreting Christian faith while respecting the Native American context.[18]

But, fourth, the many tongues of Pentecost also open up to many missionary practices. I base this on the cultural-linguistic model that correlates human languages with whole forms of life. This means that different tongues emerge out of and shape a diverse set of cultural and even religious practices. From this pentecostal and pneumatological insight, then, a postcolonial theology of mission embraces, enables, and empowers a plurality of missionary modes of engagement. Shanta Premawardhana's insights regarding the *missio humanitatis* highlight the need for a diversity of approaches in light of the many different ills that plague humankind, and the divergent conditions from out of which we all need salvation. Whatever eschatological salvation consists of is at least in part continuous with our experience of salvation, healing, wholeness, reconciliation, and forgiveness in the present life. We need to creatively participate in the work of the Spirit to develop many more liturgical forms and other social practices that can facilitate the healing and salvation needed to respond to the reprehensible mission history of Jamestown. On these matters, Native American input is not optional, but essential.[19]

Finally, then, a postcolonial theology of mission after Jamestown cannot but emphasize a genuinely dialogical (Burrows) mutuality between Christianity and Native America. I have called for such under

18. For a parallel hermeneutical project, see Pablo Richard, "Indigenous Biblical Hermeneutics: God's Revelation in Native Religions and the Bible (after 500 Years of Domination)," in *Text and Experience: Towards a Cultural Exegesis of the Bible*, ed. Daniel Smith-Christopher (Sheffield, UK: Sheffield, 1995) 260–75.

19. See, e.g., Teri Brewer, "Touching the Past, Teaching Ways Forward: The American Indian Powwow," in *Indigenous Religions: A Companion*, ed. Graham Harvey (New York: Cassell, 2000) 255–68.

the rubric of a pneumatological theology of hospitality that follows the ways of the Spirit wherever the Spirit goes. In such a journeying missiology, Christians are no longer in control; rather than only being hosts to Native Americans, Christians are just as often, if not more so, guests in what is still a New World.[20] To be sure, the Christian impact on the Americas cannot be discounted and we cannot return to the days before Columbus. However, the time has come for the Native American voice and perspective to be registered on the form of life we call Christianity in North America. A truly indigenous and contextual theology is not only a Native American Christian theology; rather it is a theology that emerges out of a genuinely mutual encounter of Christianity and Native American culture, tradition, and spirituality. We have barely begun such a conversation simply because Christians have not perceived of themselves as guests in a strange land being hosted by others. But following the biblical metanarrative, Christians can never be completely at home. Instead, we can always only be exiles in diaspora, always only be "strangers and foreigners on the earth" (Heb 11:13) who are looking for a homeland in another city. From this perspective, Christians are guests to others in their following in the footsteps of Christ,[21] who went forth into a strange and far country, and in their being carried by the Spirit, who has been poured out indeed upon all flesh, even to the ends of the earth.

Neither this concluding essay nor this book pretends to present the "final answer" to the question, Whither missiology after Jamestown? Rather, both my reflections as well as those of the contributors above merely seek to confront the hard questions of Christian mission in our pluralistic historical context. Perhaps some of the proposals in these pages will survive the test of time; they are at least presented in this spirit of humble anticipation.[22]

---

20. Here, and below, I draw from John Howard Yoder's post-Christendom theology of exile in which he calls for Christians to cease striving to "be in charge"; see Yoder's *The Jewish-Christian Schism Revisited*, ed. Michael G. Cartwright and Peter Ochs (Grand Rapids: Eerdmans, 2003) esp. ch. 9, titled, "On Not Being in Charge." Cf. also further discussion and application of Yoder's diasporic theology in my *In the Days of Caesar: Pentecostalism and Political Theology* (Grand Rapids: Eerdmans, 2010) 5.2.1.

21. See here Enyi Ben Udho, *Guest Christology: An Interpretative View of the Christological Problem in Africa* (New York: Peter Lang, 1988).

22. Thanks to my graduate assistant Timothy Lim Teck Ngern for proofreading this essay; needless to say, I take full responsibility for the infelicities that remain.

# Contributors

J. L. CORKY ALEXANDER Jr. (DMiss, Fuller Theological Seminary) is adjunct faculty at Patten University, Oakland, California, and the Pentecostal Theological Seminary, Cleveland, Tennessee.

EDWARD L. BOND (PhD, Louisiana State University) is Professor of History at Alabama A & M University, Normal, Alabama, Editor-in-Chief of *Anglican and Episcopal History*, and Visiting Assistant Professor in Church History, The School of Theology, The University of the South, Sewanee, Tennessee.

WILLIAM R. BURROWS (PhD, University of Chicago) is managing editor emeritus, Orbis Books, and Research Professor of Missiology at New York Theological Seminary, New York City.

BARBARA ALICE MANN (PhD, University of Toledo) is a Lecturer at The University of Toledo, Toledo, Ohio, a community-recognized Ohio Bear Clan Seneca, and the Northern Director of the Native American Alliance of Ohio.

ROBERT J. MILLER (JD, Lewis & Clark Law School) is a citizen of the Eastern Shawnee Tribe of Oklahoma, Chief Justice of the court of appeals of the Grand Ronde Tribe, and Professor at Lewis & Clark Law School, Portland, Oregon.

SHANTA PREMAWARDHANA (PhD, Northwestern University) is Director of the Program on Inter-religious Dialogue and Cooperation of the *World Council* of Churches, Geneva, Switzerland.

TINK TINKER (PhD, Graduate Theological Union) is a member of the wazhazhe, Osage Nation, and Clifford Baldridge Professor of American

Indian Cultures and Religious Traditions at Iliff School of Theology, Denver, Colorado.

RICHARD TWISS (DMiss. candidate, Asbury Theological Seminary) is a citizen of the Sicangu Band of the Rosebud Lakota/Sioux Tribe, and founder of Wiconi International, Vancouver, Washington.

RICHARD E. WALDROP (DMiss., Fuller Theological Seminary) is Missionary Educator with Church of God World Missions, Cleveland, Tennessee, and adjunct professor of World Mission and Evangelism, Church of God Theological Seminary, Cleveland, Tennessee.

AMOS YONG (PhD, Boston University) is J. Rodman Williams Professor of Theology, Regent University School of Divinity, Virginia Beach, Virginia.

BARBARA BROWN ZIKMUND (PhD, Duke University) is former president of Hartford Seminary, Hartford, Connecticut; she served as chair of the Interfaith Relations Commission of the National Council of Churches for eight years.

# Author Index

# Author Index

# Subject Index

# Subject Index